EMBRACE CHANGE

Flourish in times of challenges and crisis

Rorisang Maimane

Helpmyworld Publishing

Embrace Change: Flourish in times of challenges and crisis
Published By
www.helpmyworldpublishing.co.za

© 2020 by Rorisang Dawn Maimane
Printed in South Africa
ISBN: 978-0-620-74544-4
ISBN: 978-0-620-77410-9 (E-Book)

www.rorisangmaimane.co.za
www.helpmyworld.co.za

Contents

Dedication

Dear reader, I had you in my thoughts when I was writing every single word in this book, mainly because you deserve to flourish in all areas of your life. John the Baptist reminds us that in the world we will have tribulations (challenges, distress, and frustrations). Remain strong, for the power and strengths to overcome them resides in you. Best believe me, that it is one of life's goals to see you succeed in all that you do. You can succeed despite what the current circumstances may be. For the simple reason, that life is good. For life to remain good, take advantage of the good, and enjoy and love life.

Dear reader, I want you to flourish, to lead a happy, loving, satisfactory, and enjoyable life. I am certain that you and I have the same goal and desire which is obviously for you to become prosperous. I want you to know that you can live a life without worries and fears. It is possible, and you can achieve that. In order for you to prosper, you should strive for excellence in your chosen craft. Keep in mind that there is a season for everything. This book is partially based on that principle. All things pass with time, both good and bad. This simply means that what you are going through right now is not going to last. It is only temporary, a passing phase.

Once you know that, and commit it to your life on a daily basis, you will then start living life filled with hope, confidence, trust, and more importantly faith and love. Also, this sparks lots of questions. Like. "What am I doing with my life?" "What is important?" "How should I live my life?" "Why am I here?" "What value can I add to the world?" Rest assured we will work on all these questions and more. You will begin to take life seriously and not let a single moment go by without moving one step closer to a victorious life. A life that will not only benefit you but everyone that you cross paths with.

You and I are born to succeed in everything we touch. The following quote by John the Baptist sums it up nicely, "Beloved, I pray that you may prosper in every way and [that your body] may keep well, even as [I know] your soul keeps well and prospers." That is great news, the words alone are fitting to the heart and mind. You do not have to question who said them but simply accept them with joy because they mean no harm. You are a winner. It is important for you to understand that you cannot control everything in your life. The things you can control, you must take full advantage of their benefits and keep moving forward.

Thoughts to keep in mind during tough times
Change will always materialize, in fact, change is one of the permanent entities in natural life, and it is consistent. Change is inevitable. All things and everything are subject to change. Nothing can come to its full potential without going through the stages of change. For you to keep your eyes focused on the beneficial goals, you must keep the faith alive. Hope must stir in your heart no matter what comes. For you who struggle to keep the faith and

hope alive, I strongly propose that finding something that works best to attain victory is the first priority for you. Allow me to say that nothing will beat your desire and will to succeed if you truly want it.

No number of setbacks can keep you down. It is not a cliché; it is the truth. The goal is to prosper all the time. Al-ways set bigger goals because goals are a way for you to develop. Goals are also a way for you to have a sense of meaning and peace in your life. Work your way to achieve the goals that you have set even when it may seem impossible at times. Teach yourself new skills. Create more room for personal development and growth. Treat all successes and victories as stepping stones. Do not dwell too much on previous successes and victories. Finish all your tasks and assignments whether big or small. Do a little of what makes you happy and smile every day of your life, if possible, do that every hour! Respect all living things. Be thankful all the time and worry less.

Acknowledgement

Without a single doubt in my heart. I say all the thanks and praise be given to the higher power for the guidance and strength provided to me to see this book through to the last page. To my family and friends. To my two extraordinary daughters who continue to inspire me every day of my life. Thank you MyDelight and MyEdria Maimane. Thanks to my mother who gave to me and my brother the best she could by raising us and teaching us to respect and take full responsibility for our lives.

Thank you for doing your best to pay for my university fees and most importantly to encourage me to be the best I can be. To my friends, I just want to say a big thank you. Where would I be without your support, laughs, and the time you took to be with me through tough days? Last, but not least, a big thank you to you reader who inspired me to bring this book to life. Without you, in mind, I would have not pushed to see this book complete. Thank You.

Foreword

Hard times or crisis are no stranger to humanity. The only stranger to humanity is positive thoughts and actions of taking advantage when hard times arrive. Starting now to practice victorious lifestyles even in challenging times is one way to secure the beginning of a successful life. Doing this will benefit you more than your imagination could ever reach. Allow victory to transform you and become blessed. When you are finished with this book you will be transformed, you will become a new person completely. Your life will start changing for the better; hope and inspiration will stir in you. You will be empowered to act and take complete control of your life. You will begin to work on the most valuable aspects of your life and above all, you will know how to create what truly matters to you.

Everything will become very simple with every effort you put forth. How do I know that? Because I read this book twice and I am certain that I will read it again because it covers the best practices of our everyday lives. This is the one book that will make sure that you live the lifestyle you deserve filled with love, success, value, confidence, hope, and peace. Today I prosper in all that I do because I read this book, I put to practice the knowledge that Rorisang is making available to all of us. When you are done with "Embrace Change", you will begin to look at life and the world totally differently because you will tap into a whole new thinking and acting.

In most parts of the world, people are shadowed by problems, challenges, and worries. This book's sole purpose is to resolve the life of worry, problems, and challenges, even better, to help you create new successful paths. It however goes deeper than that, it does not only help you to overcome your challenges, it allows you to start creating what matters to you. To see things as they really are, to help you gain perspective and clarity when navigating through life. It helps you to discover who you are and manifest your full potentials.

It is important for you dear reader to take this book as a living entity and an inspiring friend and not a set of advice about how to live right and successful. Take what you understand, use it the best way you can with your unique skills, questioning your actions and thoughts for the sake of creating better ones. Also, it is important to research areas of your interests as you read for a better understanding. Giving rules, advice, or the right ways of living is the last thing the author has in mind. I know from experience that there is no one way to a great living. The world is filled with great individuals with each and every single one of them having great knowledge, talents, gifts, and skills that can equip them to do better. Therefore, learn from this book as I have learned from others. Not rules, not advise, but simply sharing of knowledge and resources. What is very important is to learn, understand deeply, and then put to action what you have learned.

When others fall you will rise, when people worry you will rejoice when the economic pressures others you will flourish. This book gives you a new practical approach to live life without worries. To live a life where problems and challenges are no longer a threat to your life but greater stepping stones which can be used to build a grander life. It is possible to live a life without worrying and have full access to unlimited prosperity. In this book, you will learn of the keys and approaches to living exactly that life. In fact, they are not secrets but known facts that are mostly overlooked, especially when you have no time to think things through.

This book is the answer to both men and women, rich or poor, black or white. It will help you completely, compel you to take action that is right and good for you. Those who receive the knowledge, help, and truths shared in this book will flourish in their lives beyond measure. They will discover potentials, talents, and gifts within themselves that can move any mountain in their lives. With pride and confidence, I am certain that all who will pick up this book are one step closer to living a life that has only great and beautiful things to enjoy. This book speaks to all who want to prosper in spirit and soul, prosper physically with materials gains, and unparalleled victory all the time.

Preface

My life experience has been the most valuable learning process and will always be so far as I live.

I progress as a person by knowing that everyone who has been tried and tested by life is worth listening to. I have been tested, emerged a winner regardless of countless trials and hard times. Today I am bold to share the knowledge and the solutions to flourish in the face of change and challenges. I would have not emerged a winner if I did not heed the teachings and advise of those who have a better experience than I do. I stood on the shoulders of giants and overcomers. This is one step that will surely boost your chances of becoming a winner.

This book exists because I know how to exercise a gift called "life". I know how to win, I know how to be at my best in times of changes and challenges, and you will also know how to win when you begin to understand the powerful materials shared in this book. My experience, research, and more of learning have thus far qualified me to share with you the ways, the solutions that I used to get ahead in the midst of what others might call problems, crisis, and hardships. My approaches are not new, absolute, nor the only best. My approaches are lessons learned from the great men throughout history who against all odds found ways to be successful. That is why you will hear names like Nelson Mandela, Cristiano Ronaldo, Oprah Winfrey, Franklin Roosevelt, and even the Christ and other influencers.

I will share with you the approaches that our leaders, champions, and other great influential individuals use to gain multiple prosperity when met with hard times. These problems, crisis, and hardships are nothing but the results of change. If you learn that sooner, you begin to realise that change is nothing to be afraid of. Change emerges, then graces you with the responsibility to adjust, prepare, learn, and move forward and above all flourish. My life experience has been the most valuable learning process and will always be so far as I live. As you grow up you understand things better, do things better, and become better, and that is called change. When you really look at the road travelled so far, you will learn that as much as there were happy times and many victories, life has also presented you with challenges, problems, and hardships that shaped and developed you and pushed you to the next level. The new-found level put you in a place where you have no choice but to seek development. I personally believe that it is these hardships and challenges that strengthen and teach each and every one of us to correct our steps when we faulted. You and I owe a great deal of appreciation and understanding to our challenges and some problems as much as we give appreciations for victories.

It does not matter if it is night or day, cold or warm. You can always do your best, recognise opportunities, and gain success. I will teach you how to thrive in the face of what might seem to be problems. When others see difficulties everywhere, you will see opportunities. You will begin to understand that every difficulty holds opportunities and gifts. You will begin to gain more than losing. Opportunities are everywhere and it is up to you to always identify them and take advantage when presented. You cannot however identify opportunities and victories when your eyes are fixed on problems and misfortunes.

Developing an eye to identifying opportunities is something that each one of us can learn and quite honestly it is a must learn. It is like riding a bicycle. I do not know your first experience with a bicycle but mine was scary and exciting. The scary part was falling and the thoughts that other people will laugh at me were somehow scary. For some reasons I never worried about getting injured.

Chances of getting injured were there, especially for me because my first ride was on a gravel road. Well now looking back I realised that yes, I fell, some surely laughed but that is all there is to it, nothing more. It ended there. Looking past that I also realised that today I am able to ride. Back then learning to ride meant opportunities because I was able to go to the places where I was not able to walk to, I was able to go to the stores quickly and I looked cool. I mean it is a big deal to ride a bicycle if you are a kid. Those were the exciting thoughts circling in my head when I thought about learning to ride a bicycle. The advantages were more than the disadvantages. I only focused on my advantages that is why I was able to do it.

Today you look cool by emerging out of hard times with opportunities and an ability to see victory where others see chaos. Keep your mind fixed on the rewards, not challenges and nothing will ever stop you from winning. Yes, at first you might stumble and fall but you will rise. That is the only option you have. We are adults and today it is not funny when we fall so no one will laugh at your challenges. If they do, they need more help than you. When you rise from the fall, you will be better than you were before the fall.

The hardships that you face in your everyday life are sometimes beyond your control. It is at this time, you have to adapt and adjust. Does this then mean you must spend the rest of your life thinking about problems and trying to solve them? No, you do not. There is a way, a better way to get ahead, to be on top of hardships and challenges. There is a way to enjoy life without worrying about debt, natural disasters, money, unemployment, businesses closing, the economy, social trends, relationships, unaccomplished goals, and other difficulties. Think of a goal you want to achieve, maybe you want to start a business or a new career, get a degree, write a book, travel the world and so on. Wouldn't you agree that it is best to put your best efforts and energy to such dreams and goals than worrying about the problems that will not last? Or even better problems that might even never happen. Which do you choose? I think everyone will choose to prosper in what they deeply desire and deserve than worrying about hard times. That is the wise thing to do.

Create a beautiful, happy life that is more filled with satisfaction and love than dwelling on how bad circumstances seem to be. The good thing to know is that your current hardships will pass, you will look back and understand that they were only there to equip you for the next exciting challenge. To embrace change is you simply saying to life "hey, I acknowledge you and choose to understand you. I choose to benefit as much from you for as long as I live. I will not be pushed around by any circumstance. I intend to get the best out of you and give the best I can." With that kind of attitude, you will flourish. Life is constantly changing, we as people have to adapt to change. Use this change to prosper, instead of always fighting battles that are of no good use. Nothing can truly come to its true purpose without going through change.

I myself have once thought that problems, difficulties, and challenges that arise as a result of change were bad until I began to embrace change. I welcomed every change in my life. I understood the nature of change I began to direct my efforts in more effective and productive ways. I suggest that you do the same. When I learned that I can still be more effective and efficient even in hard times, I became very bold and never wasted a single day and effort in trying to fight off or solve problems that are simply here to help me get to the next phase of life. Yes, there are events and problems that are life-threatening, but rest assured that in all you can still conquer and be happy.

I am excited to work with you through this book, surely we will definitely learn to create the life we value, work on the things that matter most without worrying about problems. There are keys and approaches that we all have to learn to live a satisfying successful life. You will learn that with me today. Our learning will cover change at a personal level, and on a global scale. I do not claim to know what is happening everywhere around the world but I am certain that individuals around the world are experiencing changes and challenges every day. I know for sure that you have great potential to rise above every challenge wherever you may be. Embracing change is the foundation of a successful life. It is the foundation to help you achieve only great things.

You will learn to:

Lead a purpose-driven life.

Rediscover your gifts and skills and use them to improve your life.

Build a winning personality and character.

Deal with life changes as they come.

Overcome worries and resolve problems.

You will create a life of value and what matters most to you.

You will discover your full potentials, skills, abilities, and learn to use them for only great works.

Renew and train your minds to always have eyes of identifying opportunities everywhere.

Gain where others see a loss.

To be responsible and be accountable for your life without pointing fingers.

Guide and help other people in your life to win. Change is misunderstood. Very often change is perceived as something that is life-threatening. Presenting permanent problems and long-life struggles that are bigger than life itself. Today things will change for the better, you will work and learn about the nature of a change. Understand that change has no power over you. That is why I believe that you should live a happy life filled with peace, purpose, love, and prosperity. I believe that you can gain financial success and bring your dreams, goals, and plans to reality. It all starts with "embracing change." Accepting this change will lead to a happy life, rediscovering your strength, skills, dreams, and purpose. This change will create a life you deserve. When you do this, you will enjoy life and financial prosperity; enjoy peace, freedom and love. Create and live the lifestyles you deserve and always winning regardless of all the challenges.

"Will I achieve my goals and be able to thrive in the face of challenges as the book says?" Someone might ask. "Yes," I can assure you that when you are able to take advantage of the approaches suggested and discussed in this book, you will surely succeed in all that you do, it is a promise. The fact that you exist as a person means that change will happen in your life, you will make changes, see changes and changes will happen around you. Change cannot exist without life and life cannot progress without change. What is your ideal satisfying life? What do you struggle with in your life? What seems to be a wall stuck in your face? In this book, you are going to deal with these challenges according to their demands. Whatever your answer may be, find a notepad and write your answers down. Keep your notepad with your answer throughout this book because we are going to work on your goals, not someone else's, but yours and yours alone; the first thing you are going to do is, put your life at ease by helping you to rise above all your challenges be it dissatisfaction, lack of peace, debt, financial lack, unemployment, relationship challenges, communication, boredom, procrastinating, unfair treatments and more.

I am no stranger to most of the above challenges. Getting to deal with them one by one led me to many discoveries and opportunities that gave my life fulfilment and meaning. I will share with you in the pages to come. As indicated above that the purpose of this book is purely to help you flourish during difficult or hard times; to create a life you deserve filled with satisfaction, happiness, peace, and love, challenge ourselves to live to our maximum potential. I believe that everyone, regardless of who they are, should live a happy satisfying life. A joyful, satisfying, purposeful life is possible upon your choosing, I will help you to achieve all that in this book. I do not claim to have everything figured out, but surely, I learned something that can change your life to live in an abundance of joy and satisfaction. Today my life is filled with purpose and satisfaction, I thrive wherever I go.

You are full of great visions, dreams, and goals and you have the knowledge of these dreams and more importantly, you have the tools to achieve them all, however you are not doing it, why? It is because your priorities are mixed up despite all you have, know, and understand? Not to worry, we will work together on that to simplify your life.

INTRODUCTION

"For a great door and effectual is opened unto me, and there are many adversaries" — Apostle Paul.

As humans, we love life which can be enjoyed to the fullest with friends, family, and loved ones. Our aim is to accomplish the goals we and life set for us. Revelling in the love and admiration of others which boosts our ego. The joy we feel when we achieve something meaningful is exciting. It is within us to want to feel excited, valued, and feeling great at all times.

One fragment of our purpose in life is to improve our standards of living. Providing for our families the basic needs and showering them with gifts and love. To care for Mother Nature itself and all the beautiful living creatures in it. These acts make almost every one of us feel alive, gives us hope for the future which gives us a sense of importance and a great feeling of appreciation. Fun activities, excitement, life improvements, and developments are part of us. When we work to improve ourselves, we satisfy the purpose of living, satisfy some basic needs that we as human beings cannot do without.

Our needs, which vary from individual to individual, are constantly changing and even increasing but whatever those needs may be, everything starts with us. We are the key to everything. As individuals, our innate needs push us to want great things for ourselves and the people around us. The reason we have people going to school, working, pursuing self-development and pushing themselves so hard to make a great life is that we love life, we care, and we want to make it beautiful. Planning and putting potential future prospects in motion is our way of living. Suddenly, and with immediate and silent inevitability, here comes change setting us back on all our prospects, plans, joys, and hopes.

That is when life takes its natural course following the principles and laws of change, giving us challenges so that we can ready ourselves for the next challenge, upon overcoming such challenges, glory, and progress follows. Sheer endurance through difficult times will make your victory sweeter. The reality is that life does not only present just one challenge to us but many. These many challenges, then force us to apply a very strong sense of responsibility. The problems, challenges force us to act. The nature of challenges will differ from person to person, families, companies, government institutions, and nations as we know. Some are facing financial problems, debt, heartbreaks, health issues, unemployment, crime, loss of business, and identity crisis to name just a few. Money is mostly the common problem we mostly share. For those who have looked deeper into life, I am sure came to realise that, besides money, there are other bigger challenges in life.

A great example of something bigger than money and everything else is the "Why are we here?" The question of purpose and also the struggle with hope, enslaved minds by the systems we put in place, freedom, lack of knowledge, sense of humanity and care for our mother nature and other oppression that are hidden by the modern world today. Nevertheless, for man to live a satisfying life, a sense of balance must be enforced, in most cases that requires knowledge, discipline, and a deeper understanding of life and more importantly of self.

When such changes come between our love of life, our goals, and aspirations to succeed, we immediately react and focus on the struggles that come with change, neglecting the gifts and opportunities that change presents to us. Some of us charge directly in the midst of problems without the knowledge and understanding of why such challenges and problems are happening. This act of acting without knowledge and understanding leads us to sometimes create more hardships for ourselves. If we do not put our best efforts to solve problems in our paths. We are either creating some more problems somewhere with our judgments and thoughts. It is impossible to run away or to ignore. In fact, the sooner we come to learn that problems and challenges are part of life the better we become. We become effective in dealing with difficulties that arise to hinder our success when we accept the reality, truth, and nature of such difficulties. It is easier to work towards a goal when we accept the reality of the challenges we face. You become more objective, open-minded to new ideas, creating a room to excel rather than playing defence against challenges all the time.

With great intentions, a fresh perspective about life's problems is needed. When we embrace our challenges or change, we learn to use change and challenges as stepping stones towards greatness. We use change and challenges as raw materials to plant seeds of strength, prosperity educational experience, and the birth of new opportunities. We cannot see or enjoy these experiential opportunities if we keep looking at problems as threats or the end of the road. In the beginning, it might be hard to see opportunities when one's mind is fixed on the problems.

It is sometimes hard to look for the gift or opportunity when our lives are filled with pain and suffering. I am human I know this, and more importantly, I understand. We need to shift our perspective from looking at what's not working and fix our eyes and energy to the endless opportunities that come with change and challenges. I think we need chaos in our lives, to give us a wake-up call to stop and think deeply about our lives. We need chaos to appreciate what we already have.

It might sound a bit odd to think about inviting chaos in our lives however it is important to learn that chaos and challenges are necessary for our lives. Think about it for a moment, do you not agree that change and challenges are needed? Think deeply about an event that pressed you so hard against the wall to only eventually grace you with the ability to grow and develop. Tough times in our lives in a very uncomfortable way may help us to grow, to start a new business, and to push ourselves to new heights. Such as to test our limits, to remind us to lean to the higher power, and to move on. Very often if you may agree, difficult times never leave us empty-handed. I am sure you have read of so many rich, successful billionaires. Great men who changed the world after facing some very difficult times. They could have not changed the world or influenced it, had it not been because of the trials that they went through. I myself have experienced the fruits of opportunities while swimming in the midst of challenges.

Without a doubt, I can tell that as much as every individual goes through some life challenges, we can rest assured that those are here for our greater benefit. That is why the aphorism that everything happens for the greater good exists. Some changes can turn into life's painful experiences; do not despair it will pass.

No matter how big the problem is, how hard it may be, trust me there is a way to get through and when we come out on the other side, we will come out refined and stronger than when we went in. It is life's will to see us succeed; therefore, it should be our will also to succeed.

The secret is to know what you want. Make a decision to win from the very beginning. Work day and night to create a life that is worth living. The most dangerous thing that one can do when problems arise, is to talk and worry about them all the time. Another is to not have goals, dreams, and exciting ambitions to inspire us to live life to the fullest. A big secret I am sharing with you now is that your goals, dreams, and purpose are the best antidotes to overcoming hard times.

How to use this book for maximum impact?

This book has two parts which are connected. You may start with any part you wish to start with.

PART 1

The first part is a little of my reality of how I became victorious in the face of changes, challenges, and crisis. I embraced my share of difficult times, learned as much as possible, and then I used my challenges to create a life that I am proud of today.

PART 2

Part two is the work, the practical side of how to win in all areas of your life. How you can create the life you want and deserve. This part of the book will require you to be focused. It is hard work all the way. If you thought, you are going to achieve a great life without putting in the hours and effort; you are still dreaming. Wake up, brace yourself, because great change is coming your way. I trust that you will find everything in order.

If by any chance you do not understand something in the book, please get in touch with me through my website www.rorisangmaimane.co.za

Part 1

The Fall, The Everlasting Rise

I looked everywhere, I looked for signs and answers but I found none. As days went by, desperation grew, my mind never got rest, always longing for peace, my heart was saying something else, it was somewhere daydreaming about freedom and the body was singing a different tune. The mind questioned if that freedom will be attained but the heart kept dreaming. Logic questioned the dream, but Hope said, "It can be done. Look!". Hope repeated, "Look!"

*It was a fierce battle among companions, the goal was one
but each had an entitlement to take the lead. If only they
worked together the journey will be shorter and more fruitful,
so the battle went on. This almost drove me insane but in all
of it I believed that there is a way. Because I believed, I set
out to look for that way until I reach my dream.*

*The dream was freedom for everything I know was in
captivity, the only free thing was my body but at times I was
not sure that it was free for the weariness from thinking,
tossing, and toiling made sure that I remember who is in
charge at the end of the day. Who was in charge? Is it me or
the everyday struggles that direct my steps?*

*Again, I sought to free myself. I looked. I again but found
none, something told me that I should take a step back and
see things differently. I took that step back and realised that
looking too closely obscured my vision, the answers were
right here. This realisation brought peace among
companions, therefore the battle stopped and synergy was
born.*

*The path was clear, the path to making things right, so every
day I pursued the dream until I realised it. The answers were
always right here.*

Chapter 1 Birth of Opportunities

"It is the fire of suffering that brings forth the gold of godliness."
—*Madame Guyon*

Somehow, somewhere someone started a rumour that challenges are too frightening, and they are to be feared. We then developed the idea that difficult times or challenges are the ends of life. When you are facing difficulties as a result of change, the first thing you do is panic and worry. I do not blame anyone for panicking, worrying, and having thoughts of fear. I myself thought like that before I walked through the fires of suffering and came out on the other side with knowledge, wisdom, understanding, and more importantly with opportunities. I was refined and here I am, ready to face whatever that may be thrown towards me. It is my goal for you to enjoy opportunities through challenging times. The first thing to do is to eliminate the rumour, then the challenges are not that frightening. Learning to deal with changes, problems, and reality is not included in our formal education system. It is something you find yourself struggling with in most parts of your life not knowing how to move on. Sadly, some learn as they grow by experience, some never learn. Fortunately, you will learn.

It does not come naturally to one's mind to understand the mess, the chaos that they are in. Most cannot understand what it is and why it is there. Those who initiate positive actions to understand what and why are very often at the advantage. They are mostly the influential figures we look up to. You will surely learn how they do it shortly.

Sometimes we create doubts and hinder our growth unintentionally. For example, the internal dialogues you have with yourself. Very often you don't believe in yourself, and you believe life is hard, something is wrong or you have a problem. This is very wrong, and a dangerous thing to think about and tell yourself. It becomes easy at times to fool yourself that when things do not go the way you believe they should go or want. You begin to develop fear and worry that maybe something is wrong with you or other people. Or that maybe God is punishing you for something you did or did not do. Even those who do not believe in a higher power would get an opportunity to point fingers and take a cheap shot at God.

The mind deceives you. You then begin to conjure all scary thoughts that at times leaves you paralyzed for days, even worse, months. Some believe that it is karma. I once said to a friend that "Karma is dealing with me". I cannot remember specifically the events which had led me to utter such words, but, hey, good riddance, my friend did not leave me to torture myself with such baseless thoughts. He grilled me with questions, "what is karma? Can I prove karma or is it just a theory?"

In some way, his questions got me thinking that why do I make myself believe or entertain such thoughts. I cannot say that Karma does not exist but if it does exist, I must not allow it to affect my life. I want to use my experience and story to tell you that there is no karma or anything against you, it is yourself. No one is against you, not karma, the universe, God, or the stranger in the streets. Lack of knowledge and understanding is what's keeping you from the progress that you desire. You are the only thing that can stand between yourself and the good life that you deserve.

FIGHTING CHANCE FOR ALL

My story is a perfect example of second chances or a fighting chance as I believe. Before I share my story with, you. I want you to think for a moment about the true-life happenings of children that are born with disabilities. Or those that were abandoned by their parents at birth. Would you say that their state of birth is to be blamed on karma? Is it the higher power punishing them? Is life not going well for them? No, they are just babies without a past or life experience. They come into this world without knowing anything. They did not have a say in their birth or conception to start with. One cannot blame them for the situation that they are in or say they must have done something wrong. For those who were abandoned, you could perhaps pass the judgments on their parents, but that does not take the reality that these children have a fighting chance in life. They will grow and at some point, will learn to make a great life for themselves.

We have heroes and influential figures who rose above challenges despite tough upbringings. This is the same with all of us going through hard times. We often create these challenges and events. You will soon learn how we ourselves in some level create circumstances we find ourselves in. We are where we are today because of no one else but ourselves. These events are the results of change. Some changes are significantly influenced by us. Unsettling changes will keep coming for as long as the world continues to exist. It is the way of life for problems and unexpected events in our lives to take place but it is entirely up to us not to put the blame on others or point fingers. This is the time to take full responsibility and learn as you get the best out of changes and challenges you face. Both you and I have a million fighting chances in everything we come across. Your responsibility is to quickly realise that you have a chance, take it and turn your life around to produce the reality you want.

MY ODYSSEY

My greatest challenge was nothing new, it is very common. In fact, most of us at some point met with the same challenge by it I had, and some are still challenged. What was my challenge? It was debt. Debt was my biggest challenge for three years. I however did not always see it as a challenge. At first, it was more of a problem that I must get rid of. It was caused mainly by a lack of financial education. I did impulsive spending and other irresponsible behaviours. The great thing is that I also became the solution to my challenge.

Debt and lack of financial knowledge led me to many days of discomfort and distress. I owed creditors large amounts of money through possession and use of credit cards, store cards, and loans. It was nice at first to have these cards in my possession and to use them whenever I felt like. The problem started when I began missing monthly instalments like most individuals out there. By the time I realised that I was heading for a disaster, I was already in a disastrous situation. I will share with you through experience as we go deeper into the book. Now rest assured and be informed that today I am debt free, all my debts are paid off. I am free, breathing the fresh air, making more profits. This is not to boast but to empower you, to let you know that you can do it as well.

You can also pay off your debts, supplement your income, and enjoy life to the fullest like I am now. If your problem is different from mine stick around and learns the principles and truths shared in this section. We go deeper than debt because this book covers all aspects of life as a result of change. I promise you that you will not regret it. You can also skip to the second part of the book that is dedicated to helping you win all the time.

You can work with "Embrace Change" in all areas of your life (finding your purpose, goals, dreams, plans, relationships, finances, career, start a business, capitalize on your skills and other life aspects that you know). In fact, it is the very sole purpose of this book to help you work out all the areas of your life most important to become the best person that you are meant to be. I did not just pay off my debts; I started flourishing in other areas of my life while going through the process of financial learning. Today I am glad that I went through such hard times, it was for my own good. I was able to find treasure in my chaos. I could have not done it if I did not embrace changes that were happening around me.

BIRTH OF OPPORTUNITIES, THE GIFT IN ADVERSITY

I learned that if I can spend money and get into debt, I can also make money and enjoy financial freedom. In fact, this is one of the best keys to financial prosperity. The ability to increase your income. The ability to make more than you can spend. Little did I know that such a revelation would change my life completely. What do you think I did after realizing such a powerful thing? Obviously, I went on to make a lot of profits. The best part about making my income was that I made it within a short period. You can imagine the joy I had, but at the very same time, I was in doubt. I mean from lack to abundance overnight. It felt like I was on the rise and never coming down. Careful now, what goes up must really come down. I did come down but by choice, not by being irresponsible. I decided to put aside the doubts and excitement aside and started using my head. The joy I felt getting the attention and the respect from everyone who knew my financial struggle. I will tell you, most of them thought that I had won the lottery or robbed the bank or something. They all wanted to know how I managed to pull off such an astonishing change. I did not blame them for thinking that way. I also did not blame them for wanting to know what had happened.

Do you think I told them what had happened? Partially I did, but I reserved the entire truth or what might have seemed like a miracle to them for this book. Most days I would answer and say it is the universe playing its hand in my finances and in my life as a whole. On a good day, I would tell them that I am working hard. You know what? Both statements are true. I worked day and night. I turned every stone under the sun to change my life. Without a doubt, I believe that I had the universe backing me up in all my actions. After all, it is the universe's way to fully support us. Look at nature, how it provides for plants and animals in the right season to grow and look beautiful. You are not different; nature provides for you in abundance. The air, sunlight, gravity, healing, and more. I did not sit back and wait for the universe to just give. I made it to happen. I also made a promise to myself that I will not rest until I am a great man. For that, I needed to work my way through. The revelation that "if I can spend money, I can also make money", was not the only revelation. I searched deeper in all the written works that I could put my hands on for answers. I sought help from others who were willing to help and help I did receive. I did a serious self-analysis and examination. I changed my behaviors and habits to reach where I am.

Today I am still doing the same work, searching, learning, and keeping thoughts of victory all the time. I did not discriminate against sources of information or where I am getting my help. If it is something that I can use to do better and become better, I welcomed the knowledge. I tirelessly improved my skills. Another truth to remember when working is to align your efforts with your abilities, inclinations, and with your spirit especially in those things that have proven to help you be at your best. Take this as working together with the will of nature. Do not do anything without consulting with your inner strengths, spirit, or will, because your goals and plans will frustrate you when they are not in line with what feeds your will. This truth is working for me; it might work for you as well. Once again if you are not a believer in drawing power from the universal forces you can still succeed all the same. There are lots of prosperous people who do not acknowledge the hand of the higher power but still made it. At the end of the day, your efforts will pay off. The law of cause and effect will never fail you.

IT IS FREE TO WIN, YOU HAVE IT IN YOU, SO GET TO WORK

It was amazing that the work I did, did not cost me extra money. I used my hands, brain and the strong will to succeed. I looked at the practical things I could do with my hands. I worked hard on the practical skills, I had knowledge of creating opportunities. I increased my education in areas that mattered more to me. My will and desire to get out of debt and enjoy life to the fullest is what kept me going. This time I was motivated by a different goal. I learned every day and exercised my mind to think beyond my current state. A day never passed by, without me searching desperately for knowledge. Especially from great men who changed the world and made it what it is today. I remember making a list of all the things I could do, the skills I have that could bring in money. The list was so ridiculous and embarrassing. Wait, was it? No, it was not. It was my fears talking me down, saying that it was embarrassing. I chose not to listen, but to see my list through without judgments. I thought to myself this is for me and no one will ever see the list. Anyway, if we can make lists for groceries, why not make a list for our life plans. The list on the next page was made to save my financial state from debt to wealth. At first, it was desperation driving me to do anything possible. I had no idea my list was my getaway ticket. I still make lists of plans, goals, and things I want to accomplish before I leave this world. It is not silly.

Make a list of the things you want in life. You will be surprised by what writing down your thoughts and goals can do for you.

Make a list of things you do not want and then compare them by making a list of things you want to achieve. Greater goals always outshine the things we do not want, take note of that. I am not fully able to explain it logically but somehow when you work on what matters, the things that do not matter or the things that you do not want to fall away. Start now, I am asking you to make a list of skills that you already have, list of the things you want to achieve. List of your talents, gifts, and abilities then start refining and working on them to make something important. Using your skills is the simplest way to make money. We will discuss the skills in one of the chapters in the book. For now, make a list of the things you know you can do very well and a list of things you have, like a second property, car, or anything that can bring in extra money. It is very possible that out of the list you make, you will begin to create your passive income or extra income.

MY LIST LOOKED LIKE THIS

I can do the following:

Portrait sketching

Web development and designing

Designing business cards, logos, book covers.

Creative writing

Teach music (guitar specifically) – never worked

I have a car; I used it as a delivery vehicle

Visit www.rorisangmaimane.co.za to see how we can work together.

Perhaps you want to start a career in writing, publish your own book. Perhaps you need help to identify your skills, talents, and abilities, and more. Through my coaching program, you will be able to realise your goals and capitalize on your current skills. Going back to my list, I hit the jackpot, web development and design opened doors for me. I was looking for a place to stay during that time. The real estate agent who helped me find a place wanted to explore new business ventures. He indicated that he needed a website for his new venture. I convinced him that I was the man for the project and yes, I was. I developed and designed a website for him, he liked it very much. Two weeks later he phoned me to say that he had a client who wanted a website. From that time on I got referrals after referrals. The money I made through web development was directed at investing in binary stocks. At first, I had a passionate trader to help trade my account in agreement to share a certain percentage of the profits we make. With the profit that came in, I paid off a little of my debt here and there and used some of the money to organize and establish my business. Today I manage a good online bookstore, and a self- publishing company with other passionate individuals who share the same vision as me. We provide services to young upcoming writers and established writers who love our services. I also assist those who want to become writers through my writing program.

WORKING FOUR JOBS IN ONE DAY

I worked day and night to refine my gift in art, improved my web development skills, wrote, and read every day. During that time, I was very fortunate to have friends. One of my friends worked for Computer Corporation. She informed me that her employer needed a vehicle to pick up and deliver goods. I took advantage of that information, I offered to use my car as a delivery vehicle, though small it did the job. The money was not much but I never had to worry about petrol. The company covered all the petrol costs. I had a full-time job working in a government institution, this meant that I had to be in the office full time. Both my official job and my extra job required my physical presence but despite all that, I managed to fulfill the tasks required from me by both jobs. I would fill in an official leave for an hour or two to pick up and deliver the goods, come back to the office and continue with my other duties. This meant I was working two jobs so far.

The goal was clear, to make more money to pay off everything and every creditor I owed. I was willing to do anything within my power to see that goal realised. The very same friend who organized for me to deliver goods for her employer was very connected. She told me about another opportunity to transport late shift restaurant workers. Without hesitation, I took the opportunity with open arms. This meant job number three for me. Before all these opportunities came my way, I was helping a sales representative at McCarthy VW to get clients. They called me a "spotter" for that. What was required of me was to look for clients and help them to fill in applications to purchase cars. Once the deal goes through with success, I get a certain payment for my efforts. I was not good at it, but I learned so much about sales anyway, so that was my comfort.

One might wonder how I got the time to do four jobs in one day. Well, it was easy really, it was not as complicated as it sounded. Allow me to break it down for you. My formal job required me to be at the office from 8 am until 4 pm that is what I did. For stock delivery, my friend would call me an hour before to allow me the time to notify my employer and finish up what I needed to do at that moment. Thank God, that time I was not attending so many meetings as I do nowadays.

In a week I knew that I will do only two deliveries that meant only two days every week. In rare cases, I would do three days. The deliveries lasted for three hours so this meant that I was absent from my formal job for two hours' maximum, as I have mentioned that I had to follow the procedure by putting in fractional leave. I was required to be on the car floor only after 6 pm and only then I was allowed to pretend to be a real salesperson. I worked mostly with individuals who knocked off late and could not make time during the day to shop around for cars. I usually worked for an hour. This then allowed me time to go home, do my reading, writing, and other things I liked before I start with my last job for the day. Whatever I did I had to make sure that by 9 pm I was in proximity to the restaurant for transporting their staff. Fortunately, I was staying in the city and the restaurant was in the city, so I was always punctual.

The transportation would last for 45 minutes because I did not have to drop off everyone at their homes. Those who were residing in the city made things easier, the others I dropped them off at their nearest transport station. I was always home before 11 pm. There you have it! That is how you work four jobs in one day. I did not do this for long, the pretense of being a sales representative ran its course. It never worked out. It lasted for about three weeks. The longest extra job I did was to deliver goods. With such small actions, I was working towards financial freedom.

The bulk sum of the money was made through web development and design. With every payment that came in, I knew that I'd have to plant seeds to make even more. I was tempted to spend it on pleasures but I had learned my lesson. It was very painful. I was not intending to walk the path of pain again. I learned to save and become a good manager of my finances. I was always a quick learner, so I made a decision to use my money wisely most days. I mean I had no choice, I created a second chance for myself, so I better not ruin it by making foolish decisions. At first, I did not keep the discipline all the times but as time went by, I gained control. This is only the beginning of how I found bliss in the midst of adversities. I created opportunities with what I already had, the tools, knowledge, and abilities. I did not have to spend money to make money. It is not entirely true that for you to make money you should spend money. It is true that some business ventures require capital to start but I know of many that you can start without putting in a huge capital.

Now, notice that the skills I overlooked and sat on top of for two years and more are now paying my way today. You might be sitting on top of skills and knowledge that could save your entire life from stress and worry (see chapter five about skills). You might have resources around you that can help you move to the next level of your life. Look and dig deeper, do not rest until you find what you truly desire. If you have trouble identifying your skills or getting a breakthrough, please get in touch with me via email provided in Appendix A. I will respond within 48 hours. You may also follow me on my website for updates about skills and opportunities.

In the chapters to come, I will share with you the great lessons I learn about debt and how to walk in financial dominion in general. I do not claim to be an expert or anything (for financial advice please make sure you seek it from professional financial advisers), I will only share with you my best practices because as much as I paid off my debts through making money there were processes involved. I had to change a lot of what I was to be what I want. You can also walk in the sweet paths, follow the simple guidance I provide in this book, add your special abilities and skills to it to prosper even more.

Chapter 2 Joy Of My Pain — Embrace Debts

I only see splendour in chaos, and I only see possibilities in the impossible — Rorisang Maimane

I used to worry about debt. I planned with and around debt in the back of my mind. I did not enjoy my hard-earned wages because of debt and quite frankly I got tired and sick of debt. Do not let debt do the same to you, do not give debt the power to decide for you, who to see, where to go and when. You might feel like that now or have experienced worse. The thought of debt alone can make you feel sick. What then? What do we do next?

What is debt? How can we beat it? I could not complete this book without touching the subject that has affected my life for almost three years. I became quite an expert when it comes to debt management because I turned every stone to see my way out. Well, it might not be comfortable talking about it or facing debt, trust me it is for our own benefit to open up and face it head-on. We must talk about it. I know that most people shy away from topics related to money. They feel ashamed or feel like they will be judged and persecuted. I felt like that until I sought help. Debt turned out to be a door opener to more opportunities for me. It could be the birth of opportunities for you as well. I am sure you have read some things I shared with you in the previous pages. I will also share more in the coming chapters. First, let us examine what I have learned and gained so far regarding debt. You can also learn a great deal from my experience. Anyway, better listen to someone who has been there.

WHAT IS THE REAL PROBLEM? DEBT IS NOT THE PROBLEM BUT A RESULT OF IGNORANCE OF FINANCIAL KNOWLEDGE.

Financial debt would not exist if money was not involved, because debt is the result of bad choices in managing money, we will have to look at it and some factors that influence it. Debt is one of the tools I used to create a second chance for my life. The aim is for you to see how I used debt to gain absolute financial freedom and started my own thriving ventures. While I was enjoying the fruits of my newly established ventures, other areas of my life began to thrive as well. I understand that for some the subject of money and debt could be very sensitive and a little scary, but we have to deal with it because your life depends on it. I have to talk about it because it is part of my success story. Another reason is that money revolves around all major decisions we make, whether traveling, getting your next business started, getting in perfect health, eating right, looking good all the time, getting an education, building a home for your family or marrying the love of your life, money is there, it is one common resource among humans that we cannot ignore. We often depend on it to get the help we need.

Money influences most of our very important decisions, it is a must that we learn as much as we can around this subject. I am sure that I have my fair share to educate you on. Let's not walk blindly on the journey to achieve great things. Embrace change will make the learning of money and debt completely enjoyable and more important the lessons will be understandable and easy to practice. You will get a clear picture and an understanding as to why this very topic deserves to be visited.

Debt is not much the big problem we make it to be. At the very same time, I do admit that it is very challenging and painful to manage debt especially when you have huge responsibilities. Let us look at the following short observation of someone who is to wed but does not have the money to pay for all the necessary resources. This in fact is the reality I have seen and heard of from people around me who could not wait to get married. More than seeing, I have personally spoken to a few who said they did in fact approach banks for loans for the purpose of weddings. For them to fulfill their goal, they always thought about credit. Instead of working hard to save and make more money the use of loans was ranking high in their thoughts as their answer to "how can I do it?". Without thinking about the consequences, credit or loans became a very good option to finance the desired wedding.

Without a doubt I label this an abuse of credit, surely others disagree however, I stick to my guns to say that such events can wait until one has made or saved enough. You might think who am I to tell you to wait? And you are right, who am I to? Take a moment and consider what I am saying. I do not want to go overboard to give reasons why however a very silly reason is that you cannot allow credit to be part of your newly wedded life. I admit that I am in no position to tell people what to do, what is right or wrong so far as getting the wedding of their dreams is concerned. Also, I acknowledge that situations differ from person to person.

In another situation, one could easily get credit with confidence that they will be able to pay it off within a short period of ten or thirty days. Lastly, there is no one fixed way to fulfil certain goals for example getting the wedding of your dreams in this regard. I am only trying to point out that credit becomes the easy way out without realizing the long-term consequences. My point is that debt can be the beginning of a very painful life if one does not consider long term results. Get to know where you are, and where you are going financially. Allow your financial decisions to be based on a solid foundation of financial knowledge. Here I strongly introduce that the abuse and irresponsible use of credit and lack of financial knowledge is the real problem. Debt is acquired when we lack knowledge of financial management. Very often debt is a term used when one has accumulated responsibilities of using credit or money that they do not have. Financial education helps us to be aware that we can get out of debt by paying off all our creditors and still be broke. Why? Because we do not have knowledge of financial management, we do not understand the laws and principles that govern money. I have a very good experience with this. Thankfully, I learned very quickly.

To give you a clearer picture allow me to share with you that after I paid off all my debts, I had my monthly earnings going into my banking account as normal. You would think that I would have surplus money for the rest of the month after paying off all that I owed, but no, I ended up with empty pockets within a few days of payday. Why? Because I did not know nor obey the laws and principles of money. My spending habits were still not on point. Maybe it was the behavior patterns that were rooted in me through years of total ignorance. Whatever the case maybe I knew that I needed to do something about my situation. I cannot emphasise enough that the lack of money or debt is just the result of a lack of knowledge about financial management. Money management, just two simple words, but they mean so much more when you are willing to understand why money must be managed.

To manage in simpler terms is to care and see to it that all goes well with every resource entrusted to you. Financial management means to see that your finances are in order, they are utilized for their intended purpose, nothing more and nothing less. You will learn that it is not merely about debt and money but the knowledge and understanding behind it. From this, I learned that it was never about the debt. It was about my poor education, knowledge, and understanding of financial management.

I am asking you to think about this, does it make sense to you that I am paying zero cents, nothing to creditors every month end, but still end up with empty pockets? No, there is no sense in that, something is not well obviously. You could be forgiven to think I'm either a dummy or mentally disturbed, but I am glad to announce that I am not any of those, on the contrary, I do consider myself to be a very smart person. Where is all the money going then? I questioned myself. Why is it going? To where is it going? If I had a million today, I will waste it away as much as I do with my current earnings. It is close to impossible to ignore the fact that it is challenging when circumstances like these reveal your shortcomings; at the very same time reveal your strengths. I asked the right questions "what is the real problem here?" What am I missing?

You can cut your credit cards; you can stay away from loans, yes, but if you do not have a sense of responsibilities you will fall into the same trap again. If you do not know what the real problem is, you will fight the wrong enemy and continue to lose. We definitely do not want that; we want to know where to focus our best efforts. It is a common desired state for humans to want to be assured of victory, be certain of where they are going, and what rewards await them. I know people who rejoice over making smart moves by using their credit. Take Robert Kiyosaki, the renowned author of Rich dad, poor dad, for example, he says with pride that he loves his credit cards; he says that debt is not bad. Personally, I avoid debt and credit cards by all means but be that as it may, I know for sure that the problem with credit is the wrong use and abuse of it.

People who cut their credit cards and avoiding loans are those who have become very good in the blame game. They blame the creditors rather than looking in the mirror, inspecting their behaviours and spending habits of the person in the mirror. Inspecting the habits of the card owner is something that never crosses their minds until the hour is late. They do not understand that their psychological habits and lack of knowledge regarding money are their number one enemy. Creditors are not to be blamed but understood. In some way it is what they do, it is their job to give you credit and overcharge you with interest. Have you ever enjoyed the thrill of getting the better of a challenge by surpassing it with something better? I have. I see debt and credit as tools to be used to our advantage now, so long as you know the rules and laws governing money. People have enjoyed life under credit and some still do. How? Simply because they are knowledgeable. They know how to use debt and credit for the better rather than turning such into huge monsters that are always out to get them. "Without debt and credit, we would not have such things as great cities, massive industries, airlines flying us to all parts of the world, resorts to relax at, excellent food at exciting restaurants, new cars to drive, comfortable homes to live in, and so many choices of entertainment."

MONEY PRACTICES – UNDERSTANDING AND ENJOYING FINANCIAL KNOWLEDGE.

"Gold is reserved by those who know its laws and abide by them". Everything in life is built with its laws to succeed. Money has its laws that ensure that we become financially prosperous when we follow and apply the laws. We will be thrilled knowing that some laws of money we apply them every day but because we were not aware, we failed to take full advantage of them. It is our responsibility that upon our awareness of the ways of money management, we note them and teach the knowledge to those who are willing to receive the knowledge. This will not only help one person but many. The topic of money management is very important, if we are poor managers of our money it will flee from us and if we are good managers of money it will come to us.

GOOD MANAGER, POOR MANAGER

The everyday lack or abundance of financial resources will in time reveal if one is a good manager of money or not. Looking at the approach of Luke 12:48, he says that those that have, more will be given to them, and he who has less, the little that he has will be taken away from him. The need to start paying attention to how we manage our finances and everything we own is becoming greater the more we progress with life. Please, the management courtesy should be extended to everything we own. Take care of what you have before it is taken away from you. Listen to your words, pay attention to your thoughts towards money, and the resources entrusted to you. If you always talk as if the resources entrusted to you are nothing and you do not need them, one day they might not be around, then and only then you would wish you had done better. By that time, it is too late. Look at your management system, if it is working well, do more to make it even better.

If it is not working as good as you would want it to, change that which is not working to help create what you desire, refine and multiply the actions that are helping you to grow your finances and your whole resource management system. The tales of old are true still today. There are certain principles that worked for the rich a thousand years ago, and they still work today. Yes, times may have changed, but the principles remain the same.

We hear that money comes and increases richly for those who already have it. This is just the result of a good manager exercising his knowledge and understanding of his resources. We hear that the rich keep getting richer. Why is that? They are good managers; they invest and save; they follow the laws of money. That is simple, that has not changed still today. It is not an enigma or secret that they only keep for themselves. Why then are there so many people who do not follow the same principles? Well, the answer is simple; I believe they just do not care despite the constant struggle that they have to go through month after month.

The rich invest, you and I can invest too. But very often we do not, we ignore the simple but yet important advice that can save us from the worries of life. The words that we must save and invest, are used very often, we hear them almost every day, read about them in the newspapers, see the adverts about saving on television and the Internet but not all of us understand the importance of the advice. I do not believe in saving and investing only for rainy days as it is normally said or perhaps, I just need to understand what a rainy day looks like.

I believe that saving and investing is for the purpose of creating riches and wealth, not using the saved and invested money to fix dents on a car, repair cell phones, or host a Christmas party. Trust me, there are those I know who save money all year round just to host massive parties at the end of the year. I do not have anything against hosting a party but consider all your efforts gone up in one day so that strangers can come to your house pretend that they like you, enjoy all the nourishment only to forget about you the next hour. Saving for a rainy day did not work out well for me. Every time I had a financial problem, I used up my savings. I would withdraw from my investment policies whenever I thought I was facing financial challenges. If this sounds like you, please stop that immediately. If you save to only use your savings when every minor issue arises you are then defeating the purpose of investing and saving. The simple understanding of investing is that we invest so that our investments can earn us profitable interests.

In my personal experience, I ventured into the stock trading field, not everything went well at first, but with help from my mentor, a very good friend of mine and other traders I increased in the knowledge of the trading world, the more my knowledge increased the more I made in profits. I am still investing hard when opportunities are available. I did not end it there; I invested traditional ways by taking policies with well-known companies. You might want to do research on your own to see which companies provide you with good investment policies that suit your lifestyle.

THE SUZY BABYLONIAN APPROACH: INVEST IN THE KNOWN

Do your homework and invest in the known, not the unknown. Talking about the word "investment" brings us to one of Suzan Orman's laws of money. She says that you must invest in the known before the unknown. Go read about Suzan's laws of money. You will gain some useful insight. There is no better example of this law, but that from the book of George S. Season, "The richest man in Babylon" George S Clason in his book tells us about a very interesting and educating tale of Algamish the moneylender and Arkad who had the desire to get rich and started with humble beginnings to build his riches. Today we know Arkad as one of the richest men to walk the grounds of Babylon. We read about his wisdom to gain riches. It may be that the times have changed since the days of Arkad, but they applied the same laws and principles that we apply today.

Arkad: "Algamish, you are a very rich man. Tell me how I may also become rich," Algamish "I found the road to wealth when I decided that a part of all I earned was mine to keep. And so, will you."

Today you are keeping what is yours by saving. Saving is what Algamish is advising Arkad to do when he exhorted that part of his earnings is his for keeps. Keep (save) a portion of your earnings, this is important. Algamish went on to say to Arkad that every gold piece he saves should work for him. Every copper saved should earn profits and those profits should earn more profits to help give us the desired riches we wish to have. Algamish left Arkad, and Arkad did what the wise, rich man advised. He did keep one-tenth of his earnings. Algamish had gone for some time and when he returned he asked

Arkad. Algamish: "Son, have you paid to yourself not less than one-tenth of all you have earned for the past year?' Arkad: "I answered proudly, Yes, master, I have" Algamish: "That is good ...and what have you done with it?'

Arkad: "I have given it to Azmur, the brick maker, who told me he was traveling over the far seas and in Tyre he would buy for me the rare jewels of the Phoenicians. When he returns we shall sell these at high prices and divide the earnings."

Algamish: "Every fool must learn, he growled, but why trust the knowledge of a brick maker about jewels? Would you go to the bread maker to inquire about the stars? No, by my tunic, you would go to the astrologer, if you had power to think. Your savings are gone youth; you have jerked your wealth tree up by the roots. But plant another. Try again. And next time if you would have advice about jewels, go to the jewel merchant. If you would know the truth about sheep, go to the herdsman. Advice is one thing that is freely given away, but watch that you take only what is worth having. He who takes advice about his savings from one who is inexperienced in such matters, shall pay with his savings for proving the falsity of their opinions."

Do you grasp the very good, wise advice that was given to Arkad by Algamish? The advice is true and sound. The above example better clarifies what Suzan is teaching when she says to invest in the known before the unknown. We have people who want to get rich really quickly. People who want to enjoy money and other fine luxuries without breaking a sweat. They fly to new opportunities without thinking twice, without doing their due diligence. Today the world is filled with get-rich-quick schemes. They are well-known as Ponzi schemes named after the legend himself, Charles Ponzi. Ninety years have gone by and such operations still grow leaving victims behind.

I personally respect the man for coming up with such an operation. That is a story for another day. Most people are aware that such schemes are everywhere, and they live up to their reputation someone will lose money. The model of such operations is that someone must pay for the gains of others. Someone ends up losing badly. The nature of such schemes is eminent. Whenever an investment offers ridiculously high returns within a short period, be sure to do your due diligence before putting your money in. Such operations will always find victims, especially where economic challenges are concerned. I myself have been a victim of the get-rich-quick schemes.

DRIVEN BY DESPERATION

With debt chocking me to the bone I was so desperate, willing to do anything. As mentioned, I got involved with get-rich-quick schemes and other desperate acts. I did gain at the early stages, yes but ended up losing more than I gained. It was a very hard lesson to learn. After the loss, I told myself lies, words of comfort. I told myself that everything is alright and that I am not alone since my friends were also with me on this. What a foolish deception I led myself to believe. Desperation has driven me to lose sight of my potential and good investments. A desperate young man desperate for a better future, desperate to pay off debts and enjoy life. This desperation blinded me off of my potentials. I mean I am loaded with talents, gifts, and knowledge. I guess I was tired of waiting, tired of abiding, tired of being broke, and willing to do anything. My willingness to do just about anything led me to paths that I am not proud of. Is desperation driving you to do things that you not supposed to do? I was lucky, I manage to get my senses back before it was too late. Some never come back. Let this not be you, dear reader.

GOOD AND BAD DEBT

Think about this for a moment, one person sees debt as bad, another sees it as good? Why do we have this dual? He knows what he is talking about. He is an established business owner who continues to inspire other upcoming businesses through his methods. That alone gives me the confidence to listen to what he has to say. Give yourself a chance to listening for the sake of learning and understanding. You will still have to make a decision on your own as you see fit with your life. Let us go back to the topic of discussion. It is important to realise that it goes beyond debt. Look at some people around you. Out of ten friends, well if you are fortunate to have so many friends, four to seven are complaining about something, maybe health risks, lack of money, unemployment, politics, or whatever that seems to be important in their lives. Now realise that the issue is not with the complaints and difficulties, but in how they look at their situations. It is a matter of perspective. It sounds simple to say just perspective, but not many truly understand or put to practice the act of looking for opportunities in the midst of difficulties. The act of looking for treasure in the middle of storms is foreign to most people. Only a few do take pleasure in this act, while others are busy keeping up with life.

My interest in reading books has driven me to always seek the best out of all the surrounding situations. That is one thing I have learned over the years from books that I have read. This led me to understand that there is good debt and bad debt. Through scrutiny and understanding, you can fully get to this awareness of your own debt. To give you some common background information learned to distinguish between bad debt and good debt is that good debt is difficult to access and bad debt is easy to obtain.

Bad debt examples are getting a personal loan or credit card to buy consumables. Good debt on the other hand is getting loans to start a business or buying property, this is not guaranteed to give you all your money back sooner but when it does pay off you will feel proud of your decisions. I have a personal experience of how easy it is to acquire bad debt. Early 2012 I bought a car even though the very same bank that financed my car told me that I am high risk and I am in too deep with debt. The very same bank that financed my first car financed my second car. In Mid 2013, I traded in my car to get a better one (more debt) whilst my financial situation was nowhere close to getting better, in fact, it was worse. During those times of changing cars, I was trying to buy a property. All my applications for the property were declined, but with cars, I was easily approved. Companies called me three times in a week, sometimes more than that to solicit me to take up credit with them. This experience has taught me that it's easier to get into bad debt than getting into good debt.

Today all my debts are paid off; I have more money in my bank account than before. I tried to get property again, got declined again. I tried to get a car on credit to prove the theory of bad and good debt. As soon as I send in an application for a car, three hours later the dealership phoned me to say that my application is successful. It was as easy as that. I strongly suggest you deal with your bad debt as soon as "now" because it will prevent you from getting grander things of good value. Get to know and understand the difference between good and bad debt.

The borrower is a slave to the lender, the words of King Solomon never gets old. According to Kenneth Copeland borrowing is one of the worst states a man can find himself in. He says that there is a better way. We must choose to be givers rather than to be borrowers and takers because the giver always has much more in abundance, which is why they give. I personally choose to be a giver. My life has never been the same since I made a decision to be a giver. I borrowed before; I know the pain of working hard to benefit the next person. We lose opportunities because we get so caught up in paying up our debts; we forget that we must make money for ourselves.

THE PAIN OF DEBT IN OUR LIVES

Debt does not end in financial matters only; it goes deeper than that. Like a disease it corrupts everything it touches, causes severe health risks, makes couples separate, people lose their homes, families fall apart, communities engage in quarrels, and individuals are driven by thoughts of taking their lives. This is a serious call for help to say we must do something before it is too late.

DEBT ON HEALTH

Debt drove my partner crazy to such a state that she did not enjoy life. She was constantly sick, tired, and complaining. Debt turned the most attractive person in my life into someone I have to run away from because I could not take the complaints any longer. It took a lot from her to put a smile on her face. She thought about debt constantly. She would be happy for a moment, but her mind was always somewhere thinking of debt. The look on her face displayed a deep worry. Worry that is not healthy to a human body.

The link between health and financial struggle, or debt to be specific is well-known. It does not take a researcher or expert to know that when one is under serious debt pressure, they are constantly sick, feeling tired and bad all the time, even worse they are scared to plan for the future. Information readily available says that afflictions such as blood pressure, anxiety, depression, literally body pains, and more are common today as the side effect of debt on our state of health.

Financial stress ranks top on the list of attacks to our health state, it may not be the lone culprit in poor health outcomes, but definitely many people feel the most pressure from financial stress. Once again, I have seen the result of financial pressure with many people, the intense pressure I felt was up close with myself and with my partner. She constantly complained. She was just not happy. Her physical health state was up and down. She would feel great now the next moment she would feel down; she confessed that she felt horrible. I observed her without judging. She said that she barely keeps up with monthly bills, she cannot provide for her daughter. She cannot service her car when needed. I can confirm that to be true because of her moods. Her situation was very serious, so it is yours if a debt is hanging around you. My examples and experiences are very light in some way. There are extreme cases where people entertain thoughts of suicide because they cannot keep up with the financial pressure. That is no longer a health risk, it is a life risk and one that can and should be avoided.

DATING DEBT

Financial stress is known to drive couples into constant arguments, it can be a pain in one's life especially when inviting another to walk the path of life with you when you are fully aware that you cannot provide so much. Why is that? Because money is involved in most of the decisions that couples make in terms of their goals as a couple. One might want to save for the future, enjoy a holiday, visit best restaurants, engage in fun social activities once in a while but because debt is at play, couples are not fully able to enjoy such pleasures. A very good friend of mine joked around saying that he cannot keep a woman in his life because of the amount of debt he has accumulated. You will forgive me if you are not laughing now, the joke was funny when he said it or perhaps it was not a joke but the fact that he was telling me all this while laughing. He said, "I cannot afford to date because eighty percent of my earned money is going to the creditors."

Looking at the situation that my friend is in, I can also admit that I have been there. You might say well money is not important in relationships, claiming that money matters not. Well if you have such thoughts you are wrong. The author of "Five languages of love" Gary Chapman says that exchanging of gifts is one way to communicate your love to your partner. How will you exchange gifts when you are "broke" and chocking in debt? Think twice before you invite someone in your life, thinking that they will stay in a relationship that is not well-financed.

Money plays a great role in relationships. When we experience lack because our money has to pay creditors, we are limited in so many ways to provide the necessary enjoyment that one needs to keep a dating relationship fun and exciting. It is not only limiting the fun activities; it is also limiting the level of security. Planning and saving for the future are part of the security that couples do sometimes. We develop and grow as a couple, and that requires some serious financial backup. We are forced to take some time away together from socializing, enjoying the full dating experience, eating out, buying new clothes, spoiling partners, and going on holidays. Having debt is not something I wish upon anyone. Please, the time to pay up and start becoming a good manager of your money is now, get your finances in order to start enjoying the pleasures of dating.

We are meant to enjoy life to the fullest. Enjoy the best experiences that life has to offer; dating is one of those experiences. We live in a very beautiful planet with amazing wonders waiting for us to find and explore; we will not fully enjoy such wonders when we are trapped by scarcity as a result of debt. I am sure by now you notice that I am trying to communicate to you two things. One is that money answers all. That is the wise words from the book of proverbs. It says in full that "a feast is made for laughter; wine makes merry but money answers all." Two is that you must deal with your debt as soon as now to fully enjoy life. You are going to pay up anyway, might as well start now. Pay up now or you will be dating debt for a very long time.

DEBT IN OUR JOBS

Constant financial stress has been linked to a series of increased workplace absenteeism which affects the performance of employees, leading to the poor performance of the company as a whole. Absenteeism may be linked to health issues. We are constantly sick; our bodies cannot cope with the amount of pressure we carry thus we fail to put full hours at work. We take time off of work hoping to nurse our bodies back to good health. While we are off, production slows down. Taking care of our debt will somehow add value to our job because we will work with a clearer mind and confidence without worrying about how we'll be able to pay this and that. We should not worry about how to get to work, what we will have for lunch. Again, pay off now.

HUMANITY VS DEBT?

In the book Debt for the first 5000 years, David Graeber says "often when a poor man's daughter is to be married, the father would borrow money to pay for the wedding and use her daughter as collateral against the loan. The daughter would be expected to report to the lender's household after her wedding night, spend a few months there as his concubine, and then, once he grew bored, she would be sent off to some nearby timber camp, where she would have to spend the next year or two as a prostitute working off her father's debt.

Once it was paid off, she'd return to her husband and begin her married life." That is total unkindness at its best work. He even goes further to say, this practice was not questioned as things around went normal, it was perceived as something that has to be done. How outrageous. Read the paragraph again and stop to consider if you would want anyone you know to experience such dehumanizing experience. That is why I indicated that quite a few topics have been touched that sparks questions and more debate.

We have to question prostitution, polygamy, and the abuse of women and men. Well, that is a debate for another time. My question is this, is the need to pay off our debts taking away our humanity and values? What will become of our communities? What examples do we set for the next generations? We will explore more of such questions in the chapters to follow. I am giving you something to consider about the results of owing someone, taking credit, or assuming responsibilities that could be avoided if only we take time to understand.

The example above is a bit extreme but I am trying to show you that things could be very upsetting without even you realizing that they are. You see because you have to fulfill demands, for example, to pay off mashonisa (loan shark) who is threatening your life, paying off the landlord who is by your door ready to evict your family out of his property or looking at the above example again someone's daughter has to be married.

These situations may be viewed differently but for the person who is experiencing them or who has that pressuring need to meet certain obligations, at a certain point, they might sacrifice a huge part of what is morally right. For example, to do unacceptable things just to make an upsetting situation go away. In some way or another, we all sell our humanity in exchange for what might seem to be our only option at that time. In a different scenario, one can steal from the poor, impose child labor, or abuse the minority for the benefit of making a little something. It is not greed (despite the fact that greed is at play in some way) but desperation that drives a man to sacrifice their humanity so that they meet a pressuring obligation. Such pressures blind man from seeing that others have paid a huge, painful price for similar actions.

THERE IS HOPE AND THE STORM WILL PASS

It is clear that the financial crisis may hit anyone at any time regardless of who we are. It may be by the economic recession, death of a family member, loss of a job, car break down, change in our salary or wages, or change of responsibilities. Whatever the case may be, this will require us to make unprepared adjustments to cope with what comes next. Many do not recover when such financial changes take place. It takes a lot for one to get ahead at times like these. "In order to make it to your financial freedom, you're going to have to get to the point where you are ready to say, 'I am not going to live like this! I don't care how long it takes me to dig my way out of this mess. I'm going to keep my eyes on the freedom ahead, not the digging, and I am going to be free!"

Chapter 3 The Blame Game

"Man is always the master, even in his weakest and most abandoned state." —James Allen

Playing the blame game is costlier than facing the problem head-on but most people do not realise that. It is easy to fight than to give up. The blame game is tough considering the amount of effort that goes into it. Those who are good at the blame game do not realise the amount of effort it takes to put the blame on someone because at the end they have to think carefully and work out a plan on whom to blame and how they are going to execute the blame, and this comes with a higher cost. Imagine if that amount of time, thinking, and planning was put towards a course that is worthwhile, the world will be much better than it is today. It is easy to get injured spiritually, mentally, and sometimes physically when pushing the blame to others.

Our emotions and thinking become so restless because of what we think the other person is responsible for. The truth is that the other person may not be thinking of how they wronged us or how responsible they are to the temporary harm that we are facing. They might not even care about how we feel. The person we are putting the blame on is very busy, working on their lives while we encourage negative emotions. It is a very common human error that we normally engage in when we are faced with pain, worries, and misfortunes; our minds react by putting the blame on someone or something - our parents for not teaching us how to hold our heads high when difficulties arise, or the environment. You do it, I do it

You look at other people's actions, words, and behaviors to blame them for the problems in your life. At times, you may start to feel sorry for yourself. Reacting in such behaviors might be common, but it is very unnatural and so much unhealthy to a human body. There is nothing natural about feeling sorry for yourself. There is nothing natural about putting the burden of blame on the next person when you feel that you have been wronged. Yes, the other person may have hurt, cheated, robbed, or misled you, but the responsibility to make things right falls on you. Remember that the Christ said even when a fellow wronged you it is your responsibility to go and make things right with them because your life depends on it. People might not know that they wronged you, what will you do? Will you wait for them to acknowledge that they wronged you? Well, you are in for a long wait if you take that approach. You might even wait forever, so in cases where you feel violated in some way or another you and only you have full control of what happens next.

THE BLAME GAME CAN BE USED IN MANY SITUATIONS

When I was deep into debt, at some point I shifted the blame to creditors for giving me credit when they saw that I could barely keep up with other monthly instalments. Were they really aware that I cannot keep up with my monthly installments? Whether they were aware or not, the responsibility was mine and mine alone. I was wrong, my financial state and life as a whole is my responsibility and mine alone. The creditors did not care; they just kept giving me credit and when month-end closes in they did not care much about my needs, they wanted their money back with interest.

Think very hard, what are you really hurting from, that you blame others for? Is it a lie that they told you? Did they cheat or break your heart in some way? Did you get disappointed in a deal you were counting on? Perhaps you did not get that job you were so sure that you will get? No matter what the answer is, the fact of the matter is that you are responsible for your happiness. You are responsible for your life and no amount of blame can change that.

WHAT TAKING RESPONSIBILITY LOOKS LIKE? Look at Oscar Pistorius, Oscar's legs were amputated below the knee when he was 11 months old. He then grew up to become a gold medallist making history in 2012 by setting a world record. His story is inspiring because he did not only participate in the Olympics, it's been said that at an early age Pistorius played rugby, water pool, and wrestling. All these sports require the use of both legs, but never the less he went on to become a champion. Circumstances never stopped Pistorius in any way. Imagine if Pistorius had played the blame game for not having both his legs. Blake Leeper in one of his interviews says that he is thankful for losing his legs because it allowed him to gain certain tools for him to be what he is today. He came second after Oscar Pistorius in the Olympics. I cannot leave Tyler Perry out; we all love the guy. What most people do not know is that he was homeless; today he is a millionaire, well recognised actor, and producer. He comes to mind when you think of some good movie personalities.

Do you think that he was going to achieve that status had he blamed the environment of his parents for not taking care of him? I do not think so; he got up and did something about his life. If anyone deserves to play the blame game, it is these three figures and truly many people out there who made it regardless. The conclusion is that a man can never move or progress from where he is until he stops blaming others for his misfortunes. Yes, there are those who are out to offend you intentionally, but if you do not accept the offense, then no one can harm you, no external offenses can get you worked up and no one's mistakes will influence your life in any way.

Chapter 4 Wakeup Call

"Getting your debt in line is an Attitude before it is an action"
—*Gerry Robert*

As people, we get carried away, and sometimes we believe we are correct in our actions. Spending money as a way to make one feel better is one of them. Very often I hear talks saying that shopping or having a beer makes someone feels better. Sadly, these are mostly "broke" individuals, they do not need shopping or a beer, they need psychological and divine help. If you can count how many times you feel down in a week you will understand that no amount of shopping or beers will help you with your worries. Let us go deeper into details. You will definitely know when you are way into debt. You do not have to wait for a lightning strike to tell you that. I learned that the hard way. Please do not be like me. Allow me to say that you do need money to live a happy, enjoyable, and fulfilling life. You will not be happy or enjoy life when all your earnings are spent on paying debts. At what point would you realise that you have taken enough or bit more than you can chew? Through my research when I was trying to understand debt and the reasons individuals fall into debt. I came across a very interesting story from one of my colleagues whom I interviewed. Read his story below without putting judgment or questioning his actions. The following experience is that of a real person with real challenges. I took the liberty, not to edit anything from what he said. The name is changed to protect the privacy of my colleague, so we will call him Theo.

Theo said, *"Let me start by saying it is very hurtful to be indebted. Before I share my experiences with you, it is important to know where and how it started. I must say this is a painful story of my life. It all started when I got my first job immediately after my matric in 1994. Both my parents passed away when I was doing my matric. My parents never had formal jobs, so I was forced to look for employment to support myself and my two younger brothers who were still at school. A little later after three months of employment I opened my first clothing account with Edgars Stores where I was given Credit of R4000.00. I used that credit to buy clothes for myself and my two brothers. I later opened another account with Markham, Spitz, and Smart Centre. During that time, I was sharing a room with my brothers and saw that it was necessary to have my own apartment to live in, so I opened a Hardware account where I was given a R20 000.00 worth of buying power.*

After building an apartment, I needed furniture and I had no choice but to open Furniture Accounts. By then I was unable to cope with paying back my accounts, so I applied for my first Credit Card with Standard Bank, later I applied for a loan with African Bank and that's where the problems started, my credit instalments were more than my salary then I started borrowing money from the loan sharks until I was unable to afford to pay my bills at all. Then followed Court orders, I got listed on the credit bureau for being a bad payer.

It has been more than 20 years being indebted but I still can't recover. Today I am unable to buy a house, a car through a bank, I destroyed my credit record long time ago and I must say it is hurtful to swim in debts. That's how I got into debt."

LIGHTNING STRIKE

Before you and I say much, let Theo's life story not scare us. You do not have to be in debt for twenty years. I can help you recover in a short period depending on the amount of your debt and also on your willingness and corporation to work. "The fear that missing one salary will send you to the "Mashonisa" is poverty. The constant need to borrow money to pay for school fees and clothes is poverty.

I will ask again, when do you know that you bit more than you can chew? There are signs to warn you that you are heading for financial disaster, like Theo's situation, unfortunately for him he was not able to learn that at an early stage. Look at the following questions below. Answer them as truthfully as possible. You cannot cheat your way out of this.

Do you find yourself in the middle of the month having no money to add few necessities in your household?

Do you get paid today, a day or three days later you have no cash at all?

Do you find yourself broke a week before your pay-day?

Are you able to save 10% of your salary?

Are you sometimes short of money to pay for transport to go to work or put fuel in your car?

Do you ask friends and family to lend you cash very often?

Are your debits bouncing very often?

Do you borrow from Jack to pay Jill?

If you answered yes to just one of the above questions, then know that you a getting into some serious trouble. There you have it, your "Lightning strike". It is a wake-up call. I missed the above signs until I was already in too deep. Good for you that you now have this book in your hand and reading it. Take a look again at the above list of questions. The bright side of this is that your money is talking to you, talking and screaming out loud saying take care of me or else I will leave and you will continue to struggle. Take this opportunity to learn about financial management, it is an opportunity to turn adversity into gains. We often focus on buying things under the illusion that we are improving our lives. That among many other factors causes us to constantly miss the life lessons that money is trying to teach. What a nice way to suffer needlessly.

We often say money does not stay or it goes faster than it comes. Well is that true? Tell that to someone who has responsibilities, but still is able to save, keep up with all financial obligations and have more to live on to meet all his needs. If you can only take time to listen to what your money is saying to you, you will then learn a great lesson to serve you good. You will actually find yourselves laughing at yourself for the little mistakes that you have made. Start paying attention to your finances at an early stage and you will never go through financial lack or debt. This will require you to be sensitive to listen to your inner voice when it warns you not to act recklessly with money. It will require you to be very observant and analytical.

Do not panic because everything can be changed for the better. Time and life have proven that struggles can be turned into victories overnight. You can create the life you want. Part two, which follows next, will start guiding and leading you out of our all challenge and worries of life. You learn how to deal with the changes in life.

PART 2

Embrace The Rise: Overnight Success

Welcome to part two of the book, you have made it this far. Give yourself a big appreciation. Part two is a continuation from part one with more focus on how to take advantage of the crisis and challenges we experience. We are starting to work now. Here we are going to use all that we have in our power to turn our challenges into successful opportunities. How long will we allow our adversities to push us back into a corner? How long will we allow that seemingly impossible problem to control our lives, to hold us back? If we are anything like most people, it has been long struggling. Some of us spend years trying to work our way out of financial binds only to end up more bound by debt than ever. Others work fanatically on marriages that, despite their best efforts, deteriorate from year to year. Still, others fight battles against fear or depression, drug addiction, or disease. Others struggle with setting goals, finding purpose, and achieving their dreams.

You are not alone: do not mistake my words for comfort but take them as a push to start putting up a fight against your challenges.

Deep within our hearts, each of us knows that there must be an answer to put all the adversities we face away for good. But often the answer seems to be out of reach, hidden behind a door that is locked tightly against us.

What I want you to know today, however, is this: you can open that door, you must open that door. Right now, you may be facing a situation that looks utterly hopeless; it is good for you that you made it this far to part two of this book for you will find keys that will unlock any door you may want to enter into, keys that open the doors for you spiritually, physically, financially, materially and emotionally. No matter how hard it may have been for you in the past, today you are breaking through, today you are winning. Get hold of the right keys, you can find your way out. You will learn about the nature of change, and problems; you will learn about the tools and resources you can use to conquer challenges. You will build a great life, good success while you conquer your giants.

Let's start working. For us to start working efficiently, we must have a goal in mind. We must have that thing, that valuable end result that we want to achieve. The goal must be to win, anything that does not seem like a winning way we must let it go. Get obsessed about winning. It becomes easier when you know what you want. Where you want to go and what you want to do.

What I am suggesting is that you should be reading this book with your writing pad in your left hand and your writing tool (pencil, pen or marker, etc.) on the other hand. Put what you are learning with me to work, waste time no more, we will take your current challenges and turn them into your glorious success. For the first time in many days of your hardships, you will know and experience what it feels like to walk in perfect victory.

Remember this: There is no situation that is impossible to overcome. Since you are going to win you might as well start winning now. There is an answer to your challenges. So, keep digging for the answers until you find the right keys for you. Keep knocking at every door until you find the one that opens.

Chapter 5 The Tools in Your Hands

"You are complete; everything you need to succeed is built inside of you. You are designed intentionally for success. Please, you just have to understand the efficient use of your design and complete form." —Rorisang Maimane

We will learn about the nature of change, and the challenges that come when change happens. First, let us look at the most important part in this book, this chapter will put us one step ahead to understand all the chapters in the book; how to implement the proven methods that work to see you to the end of the finish line. Winning is guaranteed. If you did not know that, good thing I am now telling it you. In this chapter and the chapters to follow you will start to learn why I say winning and becoming successful is a sure thing.

Everything is possible; we just have to give our best time and effort to see the desired end results. Listen, I am not saying it will always be easy, but with the right mindset and the right tools, you can get through anything when you have the will to. There will be tough days; there will be easy days, but on both days, you must keep going, keep adding to your benefits. Make the right decisions and never waste time on things that do not get you one step closer to your goal or desired end results.

Everything you need to succeed has already been given to you freely. That is the truth and the most important thing for you to know. When I discovered this, I became very confident and thankful. The revelation was so exciting that I celebrated like I found a bag of gold under my bed after a very pleasant dream. The greatest things about resources are that they do not discriminate by choosing certain people over others. This simply implies that we choose our resources. Some resources are free; some we pay for. Let us look at the tools in our hands for you to understand my excitement.

YOUR BODY

Annette Prehn & Kjeld Fredens authors of, "Play your Brain "say that bodily awareness and adeptness are at the very foundation of success. The body we live in is a tool, not just any tool but the most special, powerful, and more important tool we are freely given at birth. It is ours and ours to care for, to nurture, and use to the best of its abilities. Our bodies have amazing, powerful features and abilities that can get us anywhere and everywhere upon our choosing. Most of us have bodies but do not know how to use them, it is like having a smartphone, especially our new advanced smartphones. I know the iPhone has more than 12 standard features, but I am using only a few features of the phone per week. Some I spend months and months without using them. Why is that? It may be because of some features I do not necessarily need. This does not mean that the phone is not functioning right. The problem is the user does not take time to understand the key features.

However, our bodies are different. It's impossible to say I am going to stay a week without using my left leg or say I am going to stay a day without using my nose. Try doing that you will malfunction.

Our body features are functioning whether you are aware or not. Some of our features can do amazing things, but we are not aware of that. That is why each and every individual must see to it that they fully comprehend how to use the power of their bodies to create a satisfying life. If we are not aware of how our bodies work, we are simply violating the nature of our bodies. We are then not using it to its full potential. We do not have to wait to be obese or sick to start learning to appreciate how important it is to care for our body and to eat right, relax, and exercise. From birth, we are born with all our senses, our sight, touch, smell, and hearing.

We have legs to walk, arms to pick up, hold, and carry. The way our body works is very fascinating. That is why it is necessary for us to take care of our bodies and us. We have to use our body to the maximum capacity for the purpose it was created for. You cannot enjoy the full experience of the power of your body if you do not understand it. Your body can bring you financial gain and good status. It is a tool waiting to be used right. Before you get any other ideas, look at athletes, wrestlers, kickboxers, soccer stars, and other sports stars. All these professionals are able to use their bodies for making a living. They are driven and focused. Think carefully about how you are using your body. Are you using it to your full potential?

INTELLECT

This is a tool given to all of us at birth. Well, if you feel like it's not given to you, do not panic you can get intellect by reading, asking questions, and observing. The more you observe with patience and understanding, the more you develop a good quality of rationalizing and thinking. Again, with a fair amount of reading, studying and application this process becomes easy and enjoyable. There are lots of written materials out there for all of us to gain the necessary intellectual capacity. Every creature under the sun has some form of intelligence. If you do not have, you can acquire intelligence by means of training and learning. If you feel like you are not a fan of learning by means of studying written materials, you are also at an advantage. Here is what I mean. There is in us some element of intelligence that lies in each and every single one of us. This intelligence cannot be explained; however, all of us have experienced it many times. When we are under pressure to complete an important task or when your life is threatened, you are then challenged. Sometimes the decisions you make change your life.

This decision may open a new world of possibilities. Our creative side kicks in to reach a solution. When this intelligence kicks in we feel excited, full of energy, and a strong determination. A good example of this is entering into a new experience, maybe new employment, learning a new skill, or having to deal with the new environment. Perhaps you are a new employee in a company. In some way, you might be scared and excited at the same time. In the environment of your new employment, you have to learn new systems, policies, and structures that govern your work and the entire organisation. As you are not familiar with these new ways, your innate intellect kicks in and you begin to learn fast, and later you are no longer a learner but an expert.

You would have not got to the level of an expert or of a practitioner had your intellect not stepped in to assist you through the process of gaining new knowledge, learning new systems, policies, and structures. Consider the fact that with all the learning and observing one must do, one must also practice what is learned. It is in the simple day to day life experiences that you realise that there is always an intellectual gain in the interaction with others, the environment, your mistakes, and very often our desire to do and be more.

USE THE POWER TO CHOOSE TO MAKE BEST DECISIONS

Choices are as much alive as you and I. We are given the power to choose what we want. The author in the book of Deuteronomy says "I give you the power to choose between life and death, choose life." Whether we know it or not, our decisions now determine our destiny. Your successes or failures are determined by the choices you make today. That one decision that you made not so long ago will find a way to be part of your reality. Look at it this way; choose the things that will make you better tomorrow.

The fact of the matter is certain problems that you are going through right now are draining all your happiness and energy. In all that you do have a choice, a choice to want to feel sad, or to complain all the time; or make the best decision to feel great, happy, and satisfied. You cannot feel great unless you start making the right decisions. It is not easy to be on top of the game every time, to always make the right decisions, but you can at least try. You owe it to yourself to make the right decisions. Sadly, what I am about to say might spark arguments with some, but truth be told; the principles shared in the bible have proved time and time again to be the best way to make the right decisions. You might want to argue, please give me a moment to share this observation with you. It is written that one should not speak ill against one's neighbour. This alone does not require debate. It is right, it feels right and it is honourable to speak well of others. Another example is that you should not be afraid but be filled with hope. These words are not harmful but good to you. People need hope; they need to be courageous and live without fear. Making a decision to live a life of hope, courage, and trust is good for your health and entire life as you know it. How can you then try to argue if these are good practices or not? It is not based on beliefs but doing what is right.

Another way is to ask yourself how the decisions you are making now will bring you joy and fulfillment tomorrow. If the decisions you are making now are right and will impact your life in the best way, go ahead and make those decisions. On the other hand, if the decisions you make are troubling you from the start give yourself some time, get knowledge and understanding before you make a decision. Make decisions from an informed position.

CHOICES CHANGE YOUR LIFE

Dr. Caroline Leaf in her book, "SWITCH ON YOUR BRAIN" talks about the brain. She says that the choices we make become part of our biology, they shape our lives. This is so true it goes back to what I just said that the choices we make now will play some major role in our lives sooner or later. I know that the decisions that we make today will define what we will become in the future.

One important thing to note is that our choices also affect the people around us. Think about it this way, any decision you make about your finances affect the people you support financially. The decision you make to improve yourself will also benefit the people who are in alliance with you, your partner, friend, and colleagues. We are all connected in some way. We are human beings; we need to work well together with others.

Making decisions is not that difficult, especially beneficial decisions, but it requires a great deal of clear thinking. We just have to make good decisions. We can wake up in the morning and say I do not like how I lived my first 20 years. At that very moment, you can take complete control to change your life. You have the power to decide that you are going to change and live your life differently and for the better, starting from that very moment.

We start by making a decision to be happy. We choose to be around people who are good for us. We choose to empower ourselves and empower others around us. We choose to spend time connecting with the higher power. We choose to invest in ourselves and start working on our purpose, dreams, and goals. We choose to win at all times. We choose to never give up regardless of how hard it may be. We choose to make it impossible to make bad choices.

I made a decision that I want to be debt-free, build financial freedom for myself, which is why today I am able to write to you boldly about the decision I made. I made a decision to be debt-free and to make money. Today I am debt free and my business is flourishing. It was about a year ago when I made that decision. Our lives amount equal to the decisions we make every day. We will not move from where we are until we make a decision to move. Make that decision today; back it up with more action every day. Back up your actions with discipline and then and only then you will see the fruits of your decision.

You hear someone say I used to smoke; I used to drink, gamble, or waste time with this and that. What happened? They made a decision to stop drinking, smoking, gambling, and engaging in fruitless activities. They made a decision to do what is right. Take advantage of your decision - making power; make the best decisions in all the areas of your life. Watch what you think and the decisions you make. Think of the result or consequences of your decisions because your very life depends on it.

TIME

There is time for everything…

Time allows us to be well organized; it gives us the pleasure of prioritizing and creating order in our lives. Time is the best resource life gives to mankind. How we use our time every day eventually defines our lives. Time will expose how well or how poorly we have managed our resources. Time will tell a lot of important information about our life. It will reveal to us whether we are responsible or not, whether we are going forward or backward. Time is sweet and is to be enjoyed. It is the best resource and gift we can find in life.

Time is the most valuable entity that we cannot buy no matter how rich we may be. We cannot manipulate time, we cannot control time, but we can manage our use of time by organizing our priorities. No matter who we are, time bows down to no man. Everything comes and goes. Wars between nations fight among spouses and families, pain, joy, failures, achievements, accolades, friendships, and everything we can think of including ourselves. We are what we are now and in time we will pass away, we are all subjects to time. Make a smart decision to have time on the list of tools in your hands. It is more than a tool; it is as much alive as you and I. Have time as an ally and allow it to help in all your efforts. Late or early it makes no difference, when the time calls out to you, act immediately.

GOOD AND WASTED TIMES, NO BAD TIMES
There are good times and wasted times, no bad times. Here is what I mean: a good time is to act now towards your desired end results. Wasted time is what we call procrastinating - putting goals, ideas, work, and action off until the hour get late. The time to write your book is now, the time to pay off your debt is now, and the time to call your loved ones is now. The time to plan is now; the time to succeed is now. Time to take massive action is now. That is what I call a good time. Now is all you have, if you do not take action now you lose the best time of your life. If you keep visiting your past you lose now. Losing the "now" is wasted time. We often hear people say, I will pay it month-end. I will do it tomorrow. I will call you tomorrow. What about now? What is keeping you from doing what you must do now? I have a theory that, what you spend most of your time on, defines who you are and what you are to be.

You prioritize and choose important things in your life based on the time spend on them. Your priorities, your life, and the events of your life are based on time. You only spend your time on the things you deem valuable to you. Time answers the question what am I doing with my life? Let us look at the questions and the answers in the small table below. The table on the next page is an example for you to determine if you are spending your time on the things that matter. I encourage you to draw a table of your own and start working out your life.

What are you doing with the life gifted to you?	
Your actions	Your rewards
if you spend most of your day (24 hours) time on the activities on the left column, right column will likely be your rewards	
sleeping	Nothing, nothing at all. proverbs says that if you sleep you will be poor
Exploring new things, studying, developing oneself	You are learning, developing and growing.
Complaining and worrying	Well you will become an expert in the field of complaining and worries. you are wasting away. you will see everything around you with worrying eyes. you will not give attention to important things because your attention is directed to worries.

Taking action towards your goals and dreams	You are growing, advancing, learning and above all you are accomplishing something that matters to you. you might fail many times but you will come back stronger with a developed and improved action plan. you will feel great when you accomplish your goals. life is filled with nothing but satisfaction, you may never taste feelings of despair and regrets. you become more alive

The above table is an example to see how you can better use your time. I use time to my advantage. Use time to develop yourself. Almost every successful person I know will tell you that investing in yourself by means of hard work and, consistent actions towards a specific goal, is the way to go. This can only come about when time is used to our advantage. Use time to take action that will benefit you.

TIME ALLOWS US TO PRIORITIZE

Look at your time this way, if you spend your time partying it means the party life is important to you and you will priorities that in some way. The advantage is that you can look into businesses or value-adding ways that involve your party life. You like parties why not contribute to the parties efficiently. Organize parties so that people can pay you for what you love. Provide some sort of service to what you spend your time on. For example, you could look into organizing parties. You could be the supplier of beverages to parties or something. Do something useful with your time around the activities you enjoy. You need not be an entrepreneur to enjoy such things. If you spend time with friends, obviously in some way you are saying friends are important to you. The same applies to your goals and day to day activities.

In my case, I spend my time reading, writing, sketching, practicing, and perfecting my skills. If I am not writing notes, ideas, books, articles, programming, or developing websites. I am planning. I seldom allow my thoughts to be lost. My thoughts always land up on top of a piece of paper or note pad or in the form of art sketches or pieces of writings. This is another way for me to refine and improve my drawing and writing skills. Sometimes I write, read, and sketch out of enjoyment. Sometimes out of pressure but in the end, I do what I love with my time. I am trained as a web developer and designer; this I will do no matter what. When I do not have clients to service, I will find new ways to improve my web development skills. I do not wait for accolades or fame to do it. Look at where you are spending most of your time and you can capitalize on it. I always say that if I spend time with you it means I am giving you a portion of my life that I will never get back. I am saying to you that you are important to me and you matter to me that is why I am giving you part of my life.

Our time should be fixed on what matters; goals, dreams, and everything that one can be proud of five to ten years from now. Our time should not be spent worrying about problems. The point is where we put our time and efforts determine our lives and end results. If you spend your time drinking alcohol and getting high or just hanging out, you will become very good at just hanging out or drinking. But what good does that do to you or anyone else?

Now imagine if you spend your time refining your gifts, planning, taking action, and always developing new skills. You will be a great person. That is why athletes work out and practice five hours or more in a day. Musicians also practice making their skills perfect so that they perfect themselves. That is why you enjoy their performances. They invested their heart and soul in it. It is time that allows all of this. The amazing performance that Cristiano Ronaldo is showing in the field took a lot of effort, practice, and time. A song that Vancouver Sleep Clinic perform took time and effort for you to enjoy it. The perfect paintings of Leonardo Da Vinci took effort and time. What are you doing with your time? You better be spending time working on your dreams, moving one step closer every day.

Arnold Schwarzenegger says while you are out there partying, someone is winning. While you are out having drinks, someone is making a difference. When you are out complaining about how life is not fair to you, someone is out there creating opportunities for themselves. What are you going to do with your time? What will you say you spend your lifetime on when the day of giving an account of your life comes? You better spend time on the things that add and multiply to your life, things of value, and great importance.

BELIEFS

Beliefs are powerful as thoughts, words, and time. In fact, scientists insist that our beliefs have a role in our Biochemistry. Beliefs can alter our brain Biochemistry, it is said. I personally know. I know that some of my beliefs have caused me to do great things so far, and I know that my other beliefs have limited me in some way. I will share with you some of my experiences so far as beliefs are concerned. Beliefs are a good guide to help choose resources carefully, from the books, articles, and newspapers you read, shows you watch, meetings you attend to the people you build relationships with.

Beliefs will either build you up or tear you apart. Beliefs play a very important role in what you want in life, why you want it and how you get what you want. Your beliefs determine how much you are worth. If you believe that your skills are worth ten thousand then ten thousand is all you will get, if you believe that the worth of your skills is a million, a million is what you will get. If you believe that you are good, then good is what you will produce. Beliefs are what set the difference between poor performers and great performers. By now you must be getting the point that your beliefs set your expectations and deliver to you the results of your expectations. This is why it is very important to not undervalue yourself. You can do far greater things. When you believe that you can do something, you must give it your best. Go all out, take every action possible, and do not stop until the goal is realised. That is the power of your beliefs; it guides and drives your actions. It allows you to listen to no other voice but that one voice in you that says you can succeed in all that you aspire to do.

Take out the trash, clear out every limiting belief that you have and fill yourself with beliefs that work for you not against you. It has been said that our beliefs have been rooted in us from as early as six. Now you are twenty or thirty, it means you have a lot of clearing out to do. I will shortly teach you how to create new beliefs. It is not that hard at all. He who believes will have whatever he asks for, words from the Christ.

BELIEFS CAN WORK FOR YOU

I mentioned earlier that beliefs can build you up. I know this very well because my life today is mostly guided by my beliefs. A perfect illustration is that of when I was doing my final year at university. I was a hard-working person determined to finish my studies. I did not realise that others saw how dedicated and hard-working I was until one day in class when we were all waiting eagerly for our test results. The eagerness was so intense because we all knew that the test was difficult, it was something we never experienced before. Everyone wanted to know how they scored. While waiting, a classmate sitting beside me said something that changed my entire life, she said, "People like you should not worry about the results. We all know that you will be named among the top performers even if the passing rate is low." I was flattered truly; I was amazed. I mean she just said, "We all know". Questions of what that meant began to circle my head. She went on to say that, "you are smart everyone knows it." That alone changed my life towards my studying journey.

My level of confidence went up. I believed that I will never fail a single module until I finished my degree. Indeed, I never failed a single test, and I finished my degree in record time. Today I believe that when it comes to studying, I will always excel. It is a belief that developed and shaped me. It is part of my life. I believe that I am smart and yes, I am. This may have made me a little big-headed in some way but it is something that I am proud of truly. It works for me. I heard encouraging words and I believed in them. I did not see myself that way, but the fact that another person perceived me to be smart was something I needed to know. It was important to know. Mine was to just live up to that idea, and I did. Today I do many other things in my life. Very often I hear the people I grew up with saying that some people whether we like it or not are going to succeed and you are one of them. Maybe it is in the way I lead my life, disciplined, and always looking for the next opportunity or something. The fact is that others had positive ideas about me encouraged me to do better. I believed that I am smart; I believed that I was going to make it.

I believed I had to be successful in everything I do. These beliefs created more beliefs. I now believe that I can do anything so long as I put in the effort and time. I wired my mind to operate that way. That is why today I believe that I can never fail; there is no room for that in my life. Do not be fooled by the saying that you need to, "work smart" because, after all, your "working smart", you'll still need to put in some extra effort to see results. That extra effort is what I call working hard. I believe in hard work, going out there, getting things done. If it means reading 1000 books in a month, staying up late, practicing hours and hours then let it be. Looking at my experience, can you relate? Do you have some beliefs that build you up? If yes, please continue to let those beliefs guide you. What do others say about you that can help you become better and better? Keep digging you will surely find something. When you find it, work on it until you shine.

BUILDING BELIEFS: BE CAREFUL OF WHAT WE TAKE IN

There is something important that I want each one of you to learn from. Let us revisit the example I gave above regarding my experience. I heard something. I heard what? I heard that I am smart. I heard that I was going to make it regardless of the challenges. What I heard worked for me. I build a belief upon what I heard. The belief was put in my head by words, the words I heard. I choose to listen and then started to reinforce the words. There was a risk involved that I could have heard something different, I could have heard negative words and ideas about myself, but fortunately, I heard good words. I heard words that gave me enough reason to live up to.

This tells us that the words we take in are important. As much as we build our beliefs based on spoken and written words, our imagination, and what we see also create beliefs. If not carefully examined this is one dangerous and important method to build beliefs because most of the time it happens without us being aware.

BELIEFS CAN WORK AGAINST YOU

Looking at the above example you can notice that beliefs build me up. Imagine now in the same situation you are being told that you are not good enough. You are lazy and you are not going to go far with your life. The thoughts of hearing these things are very discouraging and life draining. If you believe what you hear - that you are not good enough, that you are lazy, you might be discouraged for life and not attempt to do anything great about your life. Sometimes it is not even what others are saying but what you are saying. The words that you tell yourself, the internal conversation you have, and what you see happening in your mind is very important. If you talk yourself down and you see failure every time, you will begin to believe that you are a failure and that will not be true.

The self-defeating ideas and limiting beliefs can come from anyone and anything you engage with. If you believe them, then you will suffer needlessly. But if you choose to not believe the limiting beliefs about you then you will be safe. Not only will you be safe but you will certainly build good character and a strong personality. If you scored low for your math or science test, your teacher will say you are bad in maths. The teacher may say that you are just not good and maybe you should consider changing subjects. Do not believe that. Look beyond such sayings and rise up. Back yourself up with more hard work. Not to prove them wrong but to build a stronger and successful you.

Be careful of what you commit yourself to believe. The ideas and words you attach to yourself mean much more than you can think. What your friend, family, and teachers or people out there are saying about you matters not if you do not accept their ideas about you. A negative belief will be that you see challenges in your life as a series of endless problems; you will have supporting tools to your belief. Your memory will always remember all the times when things went sour for you. Even in small challenges like having a car break down, you will automatically associate that with a long-rooted belief that everything in your life goes sour all the time.

Look closely into your circle of friends, do you know of anyone who is always complaining about how bad their lives are? Or someone always says it's difficult, I cannot do this or that, it is pointless to try because I always fail? See how your mood changes by just remembering their negativity. That is how powerful beliefs can make you feel, even beliefs that are not yours can distract you. No one wants to be around people who always see life like a dark cloud, always complaining.

Look into your beliefs and see what long-rooted negative views you hold. Change them to improve your life. You will not only be improving your life but the lives of everyone around you. Your beliefs can be altered. You can develop, create, or learn new beliefs about yourself and what happens around you. Take advantage of the power of your imagination. Care enough to make changes that matter most to you. We heard of people who made miraculous changes with their lives. I believe that their belief system is responsible for the most part of their changes. Write your new beliefs down, commit them to your memory, and commit them to your soul and spirit. Let your new beliefs about success, love, life, your abilities, your potentials, and everything around you take over. It is easy but it will take time. I believe you can do it. You also have to Believe and act upon it.

SKILLS

Someone is ready to pay for your skills. Your skills are worth something good when improved and used for their intended purposes. We all have skills, short, tall, white, black, disabled, or able we each possess great skills. You are probably saying, but I do not have skills. Well if that is your thinking, I take pleasure to tell you that it is not true. You have made it this far because of certain skills. Without a doubt, I know that you have gone through some difficult times at some point in your life in some way or the other, and because you did, you still here trying. It means that you must have certain skills; those are the skills you have used to get through difficult times even if you did not take notice of it. If you are still in disbelief well, I have more good news. Skills can be learned.

You can learn new skills, no excuses. For example, for you to get through some difficult times you need to listen to advice. You need to think, create, and interpret information presented to you as solutions. Doing that requires some skills. Being patient, listening, learning, thinking, or interpreting information, is all skills. Such skills are called meta-skills. The skills which we all possess can be used anytime. Skills like writing, communicating, computer literacy, web development, and many more are learned. If you are serious, you can easily identify a skill you want, work on the skill to enhance it, and become a very efficient and productive person. Your skills will not only build up your character, get you through difficult times, but they'll help you to reach your goals.

When both generic and specializing skills are unified, a superhuman is created. By that I mean businesses, opportunities are created, unemployment decreases, families are fed and lots of breakthroughs are made. I know of a man who got laid off at work, he opened a workshop for repairing and fixing cars at his home. His home gave him an advantage of rent-free space for starters. Six months later he expanded his business to panel beating and installing security and sound systems to people's cars. He established all this by using his generic skills and specialized skills. Please do not say you do not have skills if that is what you believe. I am telling you again that you are wrong. Remember that if you do not have skills, you can always learn them. You do not have to go to school for years and years to learn skills. You can learn skills by means of practice perhaps being an apprentice. The skills that you invested in will pay you a very considerable amount of money. You just have to work on your skills. Work on advertising your work doing it with passion, and then the money will start coming in. It is that easy, yes.

Your full commitment and the discipline and patience to not give up shows how determined you are. Some of your skills can bring money while you are sitting. When you are done with your learning and apprenticeship, a good way for you to excel more is to teach what you know, you can perhaps teach art, coach leaders, teach about business start-ups, writing, and more. There is a lot that we can do. Remember that someone somewhere is also looking to improve in what they do. How amazing it will be if you are just the person to help those who are in need to improve their skills!

SKILLS SAVED MY LIFE

I am living proof of a person transformed by skills and basic hard work. From despair, financial lack, and frustrations, to focus, determination, motivation, rewards, financial abundance, and satisfaction. My entire life today can be summarized as follows "Work hard and improve my hard work". The key here is skills. I simply cannot see myself working without skill or having a skill without working. There is a strong relationship between skills and work that will surely yield the best results for your life when once you understand. Even better, pay-day is never far when your skills are being used to serve or improve someone's life or business. It is impossible for you to work on improving your skills and not enjoy peace, growth, and satisfaction. You will automatically become a better person; your relationships will get better (I have no scientific proof of this but I have experienced it and still do). Your communication improves, you speak the truth and more importantly, you no longer tolerate nonsense. You become a better leader/employer/employee and entrepreneur.

MY FINDINGS AND LESSONS ARE:

Skills take time to develop and master (The fact is you will forever be learning and improving, and that is OK because you are living up to the laws of your nature) You need skills in everything you need to do and in all areas of your life.

Do not overlook your experience; or education. You will not get what you want all the time. You will always change your mind. Learn and improve every day.

You cannot afford to waste time.

You will no longer be carried away by pity pleasures.

You attain satisfaction.

You stand a better chance of getting paid.

You become best friends with opportunities.

Of course, in all the above having any skill is not enough, it is important to pay very close attention to the skill you choose. Also, be mindful of what you want your skills to serve you with. Skills for getting employment are not as much different from skills to start a business but because of systems put in place the skill that you have cannot necessarily get you employed but can help you start a business or the other way around. I will also not leave out the fact that with skills communities and countries thrive. You can make a huge difference with your skills. Dedicate the entire year to yourself, pick one or two skills that you know you can give your best at, do your best at it and improve every day. Make up your mind to revisit your dreams, goals, and experiences, learn as much as you can out of every task or event that takes place in your life. Be your own police until you catch yourself in a space where you understand your strengths and you are addicted to success and development. In your strengths and activities, you are sure to find a breakthrough and success.

REMEMBER WHERE WE COME FROM
Let us go back to the beginning, right from the start or at least 600 million years ago. Our forefathers knew that for them to survive

and get better they'd have to use everything they had when they first walked the lands of East Africa. Allow me to skip the historical details, and say that for our forefathers to survive, eat, and build they had no other choice but to use skill, creativity, and lots of exploring. First, the use of the mind was key, they had to observe, learn, apply, adapt, and more importantly create. There was nothing miraculous about this process. For them to eat skill and use of their innate abilities were key.

The power to observe, learn, create, improve, and the desire to improved circumstances are some of the gifts bequeathed to us from birth. Why then do we not use them to create the life that we deserve? Use them to build better. Each of us has survival traits and we have the power to create just as our forefathers created the lands we walk on today. The technology, structures, and science you see around have always been there, we just improved and build on what was already here. We all have been in deep privilege, given awesome talents, opportunities, intelligence, skills, and powers to mold life the way we see fit. The more we use these gifts there more we grow and others benefit from our efforts. It goes without saying that the less we use our gifts the less our chances become to attain better improvements.

From hunting to farming and to the Industrial Age and to the now, intellectual, and information age. The things that are common in all these ages are skills development and the ability to create from available resources. We are constantly evolving, our brains are in a constant learning process, developing and growing as we apply the knowledge. This is what we need today, take time to learn about your abilities, create opportunities by using what you already possess, and plow the land until you see the harvest.

FOUR (4) MUST HAVE SKILLS
This section puts emphasis on the skills that one should have to get ahead in life.

META-SKILLS

Meta-skills are the innate skills we all possess which allow us to adjust and manage other specific skills. Examples of meta-skills are the ability to think and work flexibly, adapt, resilience, have vision, creativity, desire, and capacity to listen. Integrating meta-skills with specific skills such as web development, accounting, web design, or mathematics will allow you to enjoy the fruits of change in your career and in your personal life. Your ability to be creative, to improvise and adjust accordingly is perfect meta-skills to have.

One skill that I recommend is the skill to understand and see things from other points of view. I suggest this because I believe that for all of us to succeed, we will one day work with a team or partner. Teamwork and partnerships are built on a solid foundation of understanding. Even better you will one day be a leader of an organisation. Understanding is key when it comes to leadership. To form successful partnerships or become a leader, teamwork will be very important to see the big picture not for yourself but for everyone who works with you and all who will benefit from the combined efforts. The foundation is understanding. Peter captures what I am trying to communicate with the following words, "God has given each of you some special abilities; be sure to use them to help each other, passing on to others God's many kinds of blessings."

Mind you, this skill will be needed in all areas of your life, in your marriage, friendships, with kids, in your employment environment, when meeting strangers, and so on. Why not learn to improve this skill now, for it is directly tied to your personality and character. Not to mention again that your success overall depends on you getting better and better in mastering this skill.

RESILIENCE — BEYOND AND BEYOND

Resilience is one key to flourish in times of challenges and crisis. It is so powerful that when rightly understood and used nothing can stop the force behind a resilient person. Look at resilience this way: unexpected or expected changes can happen, and it can be good or it can be a test. When faced with such you must acknowledge your reality, learn, and work it out to get ahead. Surely you will make a mistake. It can even get better if you get things right in your first try. In both cases learn, adjust, and instead of going back to how things were.

Be determined to grow a bit further by moving beyond the state of resilience. We will call this state, "resilience and beyond" meaning that instead of merely adjusting and bouncing back to the circumstances you were in before, you begin to create the circumstances you want. You create what matters to you. Doing things that way has proven to me to be the best in all possible ways. Looking at my financial predicament I could have paid off my debt and pursued nothing. I knew better and I wanted better. My only option was to move far beyond the current condition of resilience. I had the will, fire, and drive to create a better life than the one I was in before my difficult times. That is why I chose to work on creating multiple sources of income for myself.

Once I started creating what I truly desired I learned that this was the way to move beyond and beyond instead of relaxing hoping to go back to the normal. The decision to work on multiple sources of income graced me with learning opportunities in areas of entrepreneurship, the habit of hard work, and more. Had I chosen to only adjust and then recover when victory was realised, my business would not exist today. I believe this is one of my good examples of how to move beyond the condition of resilience (bouncing back). Make no room for bouncing back but be forever growing and beyond. In all areas always seek to do more than what is required. Be resilient and beyond always, do not tolerate the condition of simply recovering back and ending there but press forward to create new conditions.

LEARN COMPUTER SKILLS

I am not saying learn how to program, do web development, build your own computer application, or something. Wait perhaps you can do that. Do you have a reason why you should not? You can achieve such advanced skills no matter what. There are basics that you must learn and know. Your age does not matter. You have been told that you are too old to do this that. No, you are not. The world of technology has already caught up with all of us. In fact, it is ahead. Today computer skills are some of the required basics to know to get employed. Author of You can heal your life Louise L Hay, started learning computers when she was fifty. If she can do it, so can you. If I can do it, so can you. It is sad to know that people today still cannot use programs like Microsoft Word, Excel, and so on. You know what they do, they give excuses that they are not technology-wise, but you will find them chatting on WhatsApp 24 hours every day. They never leave their phones, but when it comes to things that add value to their lives, they give excuses. You better watch what you do. Computers are not scary at all. When it is sitting there you simply ask a person next to you to show you how to switch it on and to start operating it.

COMMUNICATION (LISTENING, SPEAKING, AND WRITING)

I am not going to try to be smart about this skill. It is simple yet overlooked. The simple part is that for all humans to get along we need to communicate. Not just communicate, but communicate clearly with understanding. That is how we grow and that is how we progress. The part we overlook is developing and improving our communication process. Communication must constantly be improved all the time. The world we live in today was built by our ancestors a thousand years ago. The truth is that it would not be as good as it is today if it was not for their great skills of communication. This includes listening, speaking, and understanding, then sharing all the knowledge through writing and other means of communication. Communication has gotten so much better since the ages of our ancestors. We can take it to a new level also, a better level of course.

More than anything we must be able to listen for us to understand the reason. Learn as much as we can and then you can begin to speak clearly. Listening is one key that allows you to interpret information. When you know how to listen and understand then you can begin to write putting your thoughts on paper.

I am sorry! Expecting four skills! I am not trying to be tricky or funny, you expected four skills. The secret to deal with change successfully is that you must create room to sometimes expect the unexpected, to be wrong, make mistakes, forgive yourself, and adjust accordingly with what is given to you. I am teaching you a full lesson of our entire journey through this book. Life is like that, you expect what is promised when life gives you something different. What do you do? Do you cry and say you are cheated from what was promised? If that is your attitude, then read this book again to learn how to deal with the unexpected.

UNIVERSAL LAWS

Someone is always here for you, always ready and willing to help you in all that you desire. The universe is here for you. The universe gives us its laws to operate successfully. We have universal laws that can be applied intentionally to gain the upper advantage of the events in our lives. Everything in this world operates by laws and principles. Some laws you know them, they have been taught to us at learning institutions, some you read about and others you can experience and see them in action physically. Some laws are simply spiritual laws (which sometimes are referred to as quantum laws). The laws are created to help you in your existence; they put an order in your life to ensure that you succeed in all areas of your life. I went on to research to find out that we have more than one universal law. The feeling was like I reached never-land when I learned that. Of course, I will only share the laws which I am confident that I am always able to manifest results upon complete obedience.

There are more laws, it is up to you to learn them as you go on. I finally understood what Hosea meant when he said, "My people suffer because of lack of knowledge." As I went through the laws, some were very interesting. I had applied them without knowing. You also apply most of the universal laws without being aware of it. Most of you are familiar with the law of gravity. Today you will learn of other laws that will work to your benefit upon choosing. Nothing in this world happens by accident. If an accident does happen, it is the result of someone or something disobeying the nature of the laws and principles in some way, somewhere. I can hear the erudite say, "an accident is an unplanned, occurrence it happens by chance" and so on. Well upon investigation you will learn that nothing happens by chance. Let us take the example of two cars or more colliding under the name accident. The accident happened because someone disobeyed the law of speed, the laws of the road, or something. Whatever the case may be, a certain law or laws were disobeyed that led to an accident. Another good example is of you holding a pen up high and then releasing it. What do you think will happen? The gravity of cause will kick in and the pen will end up on the ground. There are laws of the spirit world (quantum laws), and there are laws of the world of the natural, and of the physical world, which you and I can feel and experience.

Both physical and spiritual laws govern all our acts in the physical world that is why we don't float; we walk. If the law of gravity were not in action, we would float. These laws can be manipulated. For instance, looking at gravity again, the law of gravity is used when flying an airplane, but it is superseded by another physical law, the law of lift. When you put the law of lift into operation, you can fly, but you must know something about the law of gravity in order to use the law to lift.

You don't do away with the law of gravity; you just supersede it with a higher law, in this case, will be the law of lift. These are natural, physical laws, and they govern our physical world. We have the quantum laws, the laws of the spirit which will be discussed more detail in the paragraphs to follow. Let us explore and learn together so that you also can change your life and the lives of everyone around you.

THE LAW OF CAUSE AND EFFECT — REAPING WHAT YOU SOW

This is my favourite law; it has hard work written all over it. This law says no effort goes unrewarded and that nothing happens by chance. The law of cause and effect is connected to all that we do in the world. It is one of the powerful laws you cannot afford to not know and take advantage of. Whatever action you take, you will get rewards for it, be it good or bad. Do good, receive good. Do bad, receive bad. It is like your garden. You plant a seed of mangoes you get mangoes; you will never receive bananas when you planted mango seeds. Imagine this as your mind. You plant thoughts of success you will bring forth success. The contrary also applies. This means whatever you think about all day will produce life as you think. Surely by now, you know that it means you must watch your actions, thoughts, your speech, and your circle of everyday interaction. For example, if you think about how broke you are the whole day, guess what you will reap in time of harvest? If you curse and use hurtful words, hurt and cursing are what you will receive, and surely you do not want that. You want to produce peace, love, prosperity, fun, joy, satisfaction, trust, and walking in confidence, believing that your life is worth it. Do you understand?

If you keep telling everyone that you are broke wait and see what you will receive. Those greetings that you do not take into consideration will come back to you. Next time when you are asked, "How are you?" Say with confidence that you are doing very well.

Your word is very important. We are warned about the power of spoken words in proverbs. These give you a chance to examine your thoughts, words, and actions. A chance to start planting seeds of love, financial prosperity, satisfaction, hope, peace, blessedness, excitement, confidence, and trust. Whatever you may be facing right now you must see yourself becoming a victor. See yourself paying all your bills, getting along with everyone, being patient, and enjoying life, doing great at work, flourishing in business, living a peaceful and successful life. You can achieve all that by starting to understand and make use of the law of cause and effect.

THE LAW OF POLARITY

This law is fun and exciting to understand and apply. This law simply says that there are two sides to every circumstance. This law in a way inspired me to write this book. When I was suffocating with debt I chose to see the advantage of debt, the good side of my circumstance which led to personal growth, learning about financial management, creating value, creating a life that matters, and establishing a business. This law says as much as we have darkness, there is a light that is more powerful than the dark. As much as there is bad there is also good. When night comes, the morning is guaranteed to follow. This law places the power of choice, and the power to make decisions, in your hands. You choose either to let your challenges bring you down or you use your challenges to climb to new heights. You make a choice to focus on the life that matters most to you. As much as there are challenges in your life now, there are always opportunities as equal as or greater than the challenge. It is your responsibility to find opportunities.

"

Chapter 6 One Key to Problem Solving — Create

That which does not belong to you will not harm you;
problems do not belong to you. — Rorisang Maimane
"If you don't create the future you want, you'll have to deal
with the future you get" — Bruce Elkin
Nature of Problems

Everyone has a giant that they must slay, to prove that they are worthy. Do not think it is going to be easy, but you can be assured that it is possible for you to win. Your giant is what we commonly call problems. That thing, that big problem that makes peace escape from you. It is true that what might be a problem for you might be just a minor challenge for the next person or not even a problem at all for others. We see circumstances as problematic when we feel uncertain or threatened by the unknown. Our experience, knowledge of our strength and our abilities to deal with situations as they come gives us a fresh perspective to overcome the problem.

We can either bend over, let circumstances get the better of us, or we can fight to the end to gain victory. When you know that in the past you have faced desperate hard times and won, the next problem won't scare you. This should not make you cocky but inspire you. When you have never adjusted or learned of your abilities to emerge as a victor through hard times, you will see all situations as problems. You cannot play the role of a victim when your nature is that of a hero and a victor.

David is a perfect example of what I speak of. David fought a lion and a bear protecting himself and his sheep. He won in both encounters. When the Israelite was facing a giant Goliath, they were all scared and shaking to the bone. No one was willing to take up the challenge (the philistine giant). David knew that he had faced danger before and gained victory over it. He knew that he had been delivered from the claws of a bear and the sharp teeth of the lion. He trusted that the same power will help him to gain victory over the giant. The knowledge of his strength and abilities to put up a fight made him believe that he will win. He did win and cut off the head of the giant. David did not see a problem; he saw the giant as another challenge that was waiting for him to gain authority and victory over. He did not let the giant push him around. He did not allow the giant to insult him, his strength, his people or his abilities to fight. He did not let the giant shake his trust and faith.

David would have not defeated the giant if he looked at it with the eyes of fear and defeat. Fear was going to tell him that the giant was unstoppable. Instead, he looked at it from the eyes of courage, putting to work his trust and faith that everything will be alright.

Do you have a giant that you need to slay right now? Draw power and strength from your previous victories. Trust in something, trust that everything will be alright, and face your giant with courage head-on. Victory is yours and yours for the taking. Problems of life on a daily basis are unexpected, they come without a warning. When you embrace trust and courage, life and all its challenges will not wear you down. Life provides you with all the required tools to overcome all giants you will ever come against in your life. The key to overcoming these problems is by looking at problems with a new perspective that is governed by hope, courage, and understanding that you will win. Put nothing in your head but goals of a winner. You must also remember that problems do not belong to you, therefore, that which does not belong to you will not harm you. Training yourself to look at life's problems as the arrival of new opportunities and growth is a new way. Coldplay puts it this way in their beautiful song Kaleidoscope.

"this being human is a guest house every morning a new arrival a joy, a depression, a meanness some momentary awareness comes as an unexpected visitor welcome and entertain them all! be grateful for whoever comes because each has been sent as a guide"

When you embrace life as it comes, you begin to understand the secrets and the keys to living a successful life every single day. Worry will never be part of your life; you will not be afraid when you fully understand the ways of life and the nature of problems. Being calm and evaluating the nature of problems with an objective mind will provide you with a fresh perspective. This will help you to stop making mountains out of every little challenge you face. Problems are not to be treated like it is a life and death situation, therefore we must stop looking them this way. I think it is very important to look at the literal definition of the word, "Problem." In simpler terms, a problem means a source of difficulties.

Do you understand that? It is the source of difficulties, not permanent worries and fears. It is not an impossible permanent wall in front of you. You can eliminate your problems. The definition is profound and can help you see things differently. Since it is the source of difficulties it means eliminating the problem will give you peace. When you encounter problems, it is very common to panic, it might be common but it is not OK. Fear begins to sink in and you might begin to think that life is not going well. How do you conclude something so big? It all boils down to looking at the absolute results that are the common mistake that is hugely made by many.

When I say absolute, I am referring to the habit of concluding that whatever circumstance you may be dealing with at the moment will always be like that, it is permanent. You battle to see beyond those dark days and make yourself believe that you are not doing well. Watch out for making absolute decisions about challenges that can be turned around overnight. Watch your choice of words. Words and statements such as, "never", or "I can never win" or "I am lazy," describe what I mean by the "absolute" that gives no room for opportunities. This also makes you check your belief system for any form of self-defeating beliefs. The most popular negative absolute statement is, "I am a failure". I can tell you now that, that is not true as long as you do not believe it. It is important to understand that just because you failed in one project or failed on your first attempt does not mean you are a failure. In fact, I encourage you to fail more often.

Absolute negative words and statements are not good for your life. For example, when you say that you are lazy you are concluding that you are lazy for a lifetime. Instead, you could be feeling lazy for that particular moment or maybe you are just not up to do just one task, not lazy forever. Do you see the difference? You are not lazy, you are temporarily feeling lazy, you might not win the 80 meters' race but you can win the 100 meters' race. You have to motivate yourself. Let us go back to the topic of problems.

Entertaining the idea that challenges and problems in life are the ends of life is a dangerous approach. You are likely to give up on many challenges that would have lifted you up. Just like me, you might have been raised with an idea and belief that problems are the end of life and should be solved every time. Some pray to the divine or higher power to help them get rid of problems that can empower them to build a great life. Let me warn you, those problems that you are desperately trying to get rid of could be the answer to all your struggles and a new getaway ticket to a prosperous life. Do not pray for problems to go away, pray that you may learn and turn your problems into successful opportunities. Pray for wisdom and understanding if prayer is what you do when you encounter problems.

Many believe that when things change in their lives, it is usually the arrival of difficulties. They automatically begin to think that something is wrong, or they say, "oh boy" I have a problem now. Many think that they have permanent problems and they begin to blame themselves for these misfortunes. I tell you that you are looking at the whole situation in a negative way. I personally encourage you to move away from such thoughts and beliefs.

Misfortunes will happen to anyone, whether we like it or not. Misfortunes will happen. I am here to tell you that you can create and begin to live a life filled with a victory during and after hard times. I can only share with you how you can become fully productive and effective in your most undesirable state. Problems are common human experiences that we all face but you do not have to make them life-threatening. Beginning from today, confront your problems head-on and be positive. It is a good way to start. In fact, I encourage you to embrace adversities because with them there are also gifts and opportunities. Do that and see what will happen. You have been solving problems all your life. Look at where you are now, is this how you intend to live the rest of your life? Solving problems all the time? No, surely at some point you must create a life of value. A life that is full of joy, love, financial success, and adventure.

Look at all the heroes of the bible; they were all at some point facing some of the most difficult challenges. Most of them went through trials that were devastating. Some stole, some were murderers and some were blind, locked in jails, and in the case of Daniel, thrown into the fire and then into the lion's den. They all became great men of all time through their endurance and the will to rise above trials. Sure, trust and faith played a major role in their victories. That is why it is important for you to also have faith. Look at the heroes of the world. Look at the life of Roosevelt. When he died the US was the richest and powerful nation, still is today. But it was not always like that. During Roosevelt's time of office, the US faced the greatest depression, banks were closing and unemployment was at its peak. Nelson Mandela spent 27 years in prison. He came out to impact not only South Africa but the whole world. His deeds are celebrated all over the world. Donald Trump was once R999 million dollars in debt, declared bankruptcy more than four times. He is now the president of the US and still counted among the billionaires.

Oprah Winfrey was sexually and physically abused at a young age. She was rejected, fired from her reporting job, told that she was unfit for TV. Now she is one of the most influential women in the world whose net worth is over two billion. We can never complete our list of great individuals without the motivating life of Abraham Lincoln. His fiancé died, he failed in business twice, and he had a nervous breakdown. He had lost many elections but emerged one of history's influential presidents.

There are many great heroes out there, I am sure you know some that I am not mentioning here. All these influential individuals are like you and me, but they stayed strong. They never lost sight of hope, never gave up on their dreams. Today we read about them, we watch them on television. We look up to them. What we do not understand is that each and every single one of them went through the fires of challenges. They faced problems in their personal and professional lives. They all have one thing in common, they did not give up. They believed they could win and they did win.

Problems do not exist because they want to destroy you. They are there and that is the end of it, you must make an effort to learn from them. Develop and use your abilities to become better. Problems exist for your benefit, to show how strong you are. Today we only know how strong we are by the problems we overcome. The problems that you have turned into successful opportunities. We can only tell how strong someone is when they lift something bigger and stronger than them. We should not only live to solve problems but rise above them to create a great life. Do you now understand why I say throughout the years we looked at problems wrong? We misunderstood the nature of problems; problems are just as they are, "problems" that's it. You can spend the rest of your life solving them or you can implement a high order by creating a better life.

THE "NO ONE SIZE FITS ALL" AND THE "TEXTBOOK PROBLEMS"

Pay attention to what I am going to share with you because you are going to have to remember this for the rest of your life. Problems exist. Problems will not ask for anyone's permission to exist. This is important to know because in some way you acknowledge reality. It does not mean you have to have problems in your life or spend your precious time solving them. Some problems can be solved by just a press of a button and others by their nature do not have to be solved. Attempting to solve some problems will leave you depressed without any energy to do anything valuable with your life. Do not let this scare you; you shall learn that there is more to this. You never look at the nature of problems and how each problem can be dealt with differently. Each problem needs understanding and a fresh perspective to be dealt with. When problems arise, the first thing that comes to mind is to solve them or even worse ignore them. Today I will teach you to notice the difference in the problems you face. I will teach you how to pick your fights very well. You will learn which problems can be solved and those that require a different approach.

KNOW YOUR PROBLEMS: "NO ONE SIZE FITS ALL" AND THE "TEXTBOOK PROBLEMS"

The "no one size fits all" problems are not really problems; they are more of life inconveniences. What I mean is that they are those challenges that you will sooner or later face regardless of who you are. Rich or poor, black or white you must go through them. It is not a matter of choice, but to face them. It is a must because they are a special kind of problem that you need to develop as a person. Some of your achievements and success depend entirely on how you handle the "no one size fits all" problems. The "no one size fits all" exposes your attitude and perception towards situations.

You may try to avoid them, but they really cannot be avoided. Some face these challenges sooner, repeatedly and endlessly. The "no one size fits all" cannot be solved as I mentioned, because we have not learned how to deal with them. We mistake them and call them problems instead of challenges. Not just any challenges, special challenges that we should rejoice when we go through them. You might say, "Rorisang, you are crazy. How can I rejoice when I am pressured by challenges." Give me a moment; in the next few paragraphs, you will understand why I said that. The "textbook problems" are the easy ones, the daily inconveniences that we face on a daily basis. We mistake them for problems instead of inconveniences.

The "textbook problems" are more dependent on the kind of lifestyle you lead. You can learn a lot from the "No one size fits all" but with the "Textbook problem," it all boils down to the knowledge that is readily available. What you own, who you know, what you know, what you can do and who can help.

Bruce Elkin, author of "Simplicity and Success", "Thrive" and "The ABCs of emotional mastery", educated me. What I call the "Textbook problems" is called convergent problems which are solvable. The more you focus on them, the more your answers will converge around a solution. What I call the "no one size fits all problems" are called divergent problems. You simply cannot solve divergent problems. No matter what you do, you cannot find a solution. The best part about divergent problems is that they will never leave you empty-handed. Growth and fun are guaranteed depending on your attitude.

The moment you been waiting for: the perfect example and clarity of what I was speaking of.

"TEXTBOOK" PROBLEMS

Imagine your washing machine stops working; you don't stress because chances for your machine to work perfectly again are very high. Your machine can be fixed. The solution lies either with the manufacture of the machine or a skilled person who is well knowledgeable, trained to fix washing machines. You will find thousands of skilled people who can help you to solve problems like that. Your car breaks down, the manufacture or mechanic can get it up and running in no time. This goes for other manufactured items like toasters, fridges, and cell phones. That is why I said it depends more on the knowledge that is readily available. What you own, who you know, what you know, what you can do and who can help.

You break your arm now; you have a choice to go to any doctor that is qualified to help you in that area of need. You do not have to stress or crack your head by that. We have hospitals and medical doctors. It is not going to be a question of "if", when you get to the hospital or to a doctor you will be well attended to your need and your arm will be braced and you will be good to go. Yes, you may have pains here and there but then the problem is resolved. Are you over-indebted, facing a dry season in your finances? Learn about financial management. Make more money and pay off your debt and your problem is solved. The above problems I never stress about, because the solution is at everyone's disposal. That is why I say most of your problems especially the "textbook "are easily resolved with one press of a button, it all comes down to knowledge, skills, and the people who can put the skills and knowledge to good practice.

"NO ONE SIZE FITS ALL" PROBLEMS

We then have the "no one size fits all" problems, the special kind that makes a man what he is to become. The "no one size fits all" can make you or break you. These are the problems that no matter what you do, you cannot solve but, you have to rise above them. You must have the knowledge, discipline, commitment, and understanding to make things right. All around the world, everyone experiences the "no one size fits all" problems. They do not have specifics. Though the principles of working them out might be the same or related. In the end, we must accept that the answer lies not in solving these problems but in seeing them through, adjusting, and learning until life ends.

For example; there is "no one size fits all" in raising your children, discipline, care, and many other things are needed. Each parent does it differently as they see fit with their children. In time, they adjust, work it out and learn to care, love, and have patience. Greater human skills and spiritual forces are at play in this process. No one can ever write a simple manual and say their way is correct. Each parent has their own way to raise their children. We know that we can all raise children, and if done correctly, they will turn out to be great.

Is there a manual or a solution for healing a broken heart, or dealing with a loss of a loved one or finding your life purpose? The question is a big challenge for many across the universe. Why am I here? What should I do with my life? These problems can drive one insane when left unattended. There is no one solution to these questions.

Learning about oneself can help one to truly find the answer to the questions? Each person is different, so his journey will be different. How do you find a perfect solution for a relationship that has run its course, or a bad break up? How does one give another solution to solve the problems they are facing every day? Again, it goes back to adjusting, continuing to live, and learn. Find pleasure and strength in creating a life that you deserve; explore. Live for a cause that will enable you to utilize all your best skills and abilities. Again, this could be different for other million individuals out there. The problem is not to be solved but surpassed by a higher order. Time plays a role; everything changes and you become better with changes. Connecting with the higher power and the universe itself is the primary source to help with the revelations to live purposefully and heal spiritual needs. This is also a case that one cannot solve because to attain such revelation you need to work it out within your spiritual man. Personally, I consult daily for answers and guidance.

The process cannot be the same for all of us. Yes, there are many ways that people can pursue to create financial stability. Some find the bliss of making money through their passions, some follow careers, some rob and steal, some venture into business without satisfying their passions. All of that and more can get you to gain financial stability; there is just no one correct way to do it. It can never be the same for all of us. If you lack finance, there is no fixed way of gaining your financial freedom. You need to work it out according to your abilities, resources, and desires. Do you now understand? Dealing with things of the spirit, matters of the heart, or dealing with nature are totally different. To get ahead in such circumstances, one needs to focus on the things that will bring worthwhile results. You will shortly learn how to do that in the next section of this chapter I found out that having problems is like a blessing. Here are other things I found out about problems:

Problems are training and arming you to be a change agent.

Problems develop you mentally and spiritually.

Problems never leave you empty-handed; you become wise, knowledgeable, and gain a better understanding to become more responsible.

Sure, you can find more benefits; this is also another good example of the "no one size fits all". The ability to identify benefits in the midst of hardships depends entirely on you. It will be foolish to think that you can live a problem-free life. In fact, the more you succeed and accomplish the more you'll have challenges standing in your way. The secret to getting ahead is to always look for the golden opportunities. See beyond the problem and continue to work your way out. Work on it until you get through. The nature of life and problems is that when you fix one thing, another emerges. The fun part is that when you understand this and accept it, you will realise that we need such chaos in life. It keeps life exciting and interesting. Preparation is all you need to do. Prepare your thoughts and emotions to deal with the next challenge. You will learn more about preparation in chapter 14: The Ark.

CREATING

Creating is such a higher-order form. It can embrace and transcend problems in the pursuit of desired results— Bruce Elkin

Your problem can be your gain. It could be the birth of a career, new skills, innovations, businesses, and new partnerships. Create change that last and add value. Problems will drag you down or build you up. I want to help and make sure that you are building up. You are making the decision to want to build and then start building. Very shortly I will share with you the approaches that will take all your problems and turn them into successful opportunities. Whatever problem or change you are going through currently I am confident that you will find some helpful approaches that will change your life for the better.

I want you to feel and experience the evidence of my teaching in the next exercise that we will do. I want you to grasp and experience the truth behind what I am sharing with you. Let us do this exercise together. Think of a situation in your life, a very personal problem that you do not like and want to change. A situation that has bothered you or still bothering you and you would very much love to get past it. For example, let's say debt is something that is bothering you and you want to change it. Take a moment and calm yourself. Close your eyes and start to think about how every month end you get paid. Then your bills are already piled up for you. Creditors are phoning to remind you of your next instalments and making threats against you for late payments. You barely keep up with monthly rentals. Your family needs you to get them the basic necessities and sometimes you do not manage to provide all that is needed. What happens when you are not able to meet the needs of your family? Focus your attention, feelings, and thoughts on this problem. See how humiliating it is for you to be working but not holding up to your own. Stop now. Notice your feelings; you might be having feelings of worry, fear, irritation, and depression now. You might be a little angry and not wanting to even think about it anymore. Stop thinking about it, please.

Get fresh air, breathe for a minute listen to your favorite song, or do something to cheer you up. Now come back, shift your attention towards something you love. Something you would like to accomplish. Think about anything you desire to create or the end results of your goal. Start to think of that goal, your dream that you so much want to achieve. For example, maybe you want to write a book. Imagine yourself every day making time to write one chapter a day. Interviewing people and reading your favorite books. Experiencing the feeling of writing, immerse yourself in research, and getting positive feedback from what you have written so far. You are seeing your book finished getting ready to be published.

Experience the feeling of your book in print, and you getting interviewed about your work, you are perhaps on radio, TV shows and seminars to share the ideas in your book. The money from sales is coming in. You are able to start other projects with ease, and you achieve them effortlessly. Everything is possible for you right now. You see the results of your creation and you live your life with the certainty that everything is well. You feel great and confident with every new project you accomplish. You grow and become better and richer than before.

Opportunities are streaming towards you. Stop and notice the feelings you are experiencing. I bet you are smiling, inspired, and feeling great. You feel that you can do anything you want. In fact, you feel happy and motivated. You are currently experiencing hope in your life; you have a vision that will take you to the next level in your life. The question is which of the above situations would you like to see manifested in your life? Is it the worry of what you do not have or the creation of what matters? Once again, a man cannot serve two masters, it's either you serve one and the other will surely suffer.

This is true for your entire situation. Do you choose to serve your goals or worry? Do you choose to dwell in the first scenario which makes you worry or do you choose the second scenario where you win all the time? I am confident to say that all of us would want to live a life filled with opportunities where you achieve all your goals. Where your plans come together and opportunities are everywhere. Make a decision now, note that the decision you make now will affect the rest of your life. Choose thoughts of the possible world where you are able to create what you deserve. You rather create and focus on the creation of a happy life than to worry about the problems that take away your happiness and joy. Remember that it is impossible to please two masters, if you are doing that, stop right now and make a choice to serve the master that brings joy, satisfaction, love and hope to your life.

We all want something that is bigger and better than our problems. Have something that gives your life hope and purpose, regardless of circumstances. That something is in you; it is that desire to have the best of everything in life. Some may want to argue and to say, but I do not know what I really want. The answer to that is simple, how do you want your future to look like, how do you picture yourself living five years from now? These pictures and future thoughts should only be positive, life rewarding, and always bringing joy and happiness to you when you think about them. Your thoughts should also develop you. Move you a step further from positive thinking to empowerment, from empowerment to action, from action to results then repeat and refine the process. What is your preferred future? Answer that then you can start creating that life. Please understand that this approach does not ignore problems or pretend like they do not exist. In fact, you do acknowledge that you have challenges, but you choose to surpass them with something better and bigger. You might be wondering what is bigger and better. Let me begin to give you a perfect illustration which will give you a vivid clarity. If you have been in a position to travel using an airplane at some point you probably wondered how the plane operates.

One- day I asked myself out of deep curiosity, how they fly such a massive amazing object. I mean the airplane is huge and yet it is designed specifically to fly. Look at the Boeing 747-8, one of the largest airplanes weighing over 400, 000 kg, that is big and very heavy but it is able to take flight. Why is gravity not pulling the Boeing down? I mean the law of gravity as we know it can sink such massive weight deep to the core of the earth. So how do they fly   an   airplane?

According to my research, I found out that since the law of gravity is what keeps us and other objects on the ground, that law needs to be surpassed by another greater law, a superior law, the law of Aerodynamics or the law of lift as some of you may understand it. The law of lift causes an airplane to get off the ground and stay up in the air. When an airplane is moving at a speed of 150-180 mph, the speed creates this law of lift. That speed makes the airplane impossible to stay on the ground that is why the plane then lifts off.

The law of gravity submits to the law of lift and the plane takes flight. The plane must keep the same speed when up in the air to keep the balance. If it drops the speed the plane will stop operating with the law of lift and will get pulled down by gravity. This is so exciting and important to know. This illustration can be applied in all your circumstances. You are having difficulties? Get a higher form to surpass all your difficulties just like an airplane.

Once you start working on surpassing your current difficulties you must not quit until you get the desired end results. You must keep consistency on the things that keep you up, happy, and successful. The illustration of the plane and the laws that make it function is what you are going through now. The situations or difficulties that are keeping you down will be the source of your growth, progress, and success when you know how to use the great powers at your disposal.

CREATING IS SUPERIOR TO PROBLEM SOLVING

Creation is the key to all your problems. That is why I say you must create instead of worrying, or trying to solve the problem. I do not know how to better explain this sensibly; however, somehow when you create, you automatically solve the problem. Creating is better than solving problems. Creating allows you to keep the goal or the end result in mind. It allows you to keep the vision and see only what you want out of the current crisis. Despite how difficult things may look, when you begin to create, somehow amazing things start happening in your life.

Creation has this power that cannot be explained but comes to your aid when you need it most. Somehow when you are determined to get the better out of your crisis and problems, the creative juices come to your aid. The problem that has been torturing you will now be under the power of your command because of the power to create. When greater expectations are demanded upon you especially by the responsibilities obligated to perform for your loved ones, responsibility to prove how much of a strong person you are, you unintentionally accept the challenge and the demands.

Your strength, knowledge, abilities, and skills increase. The better you become and the better your life flourishes. Problems help people to create and add value to life. I am under the impression that you understand now that you do not have to spend time dwelling on the problem. You must create what matters to live a productive, successful, and happy life.

When you do this, you will then begin to see your problem with a different eye. You will begin to see your problems as challenges, you will use the same challenges to motivate yourself, to build up and flourish. You will come up and create new ways to resolve your problems. The idea is to shift your focus and best efforts to a more fulfilling and productive state of mind. I understand that it is not easy to do this when you are in a grieving or worrying situation. It will take time to shift from your old way of seeing things to the new ways, but it is not impossible. With the right mind and discipline, you can do it.

Creating is one of the best ways to beat adversities. It is your responsibility to always seek to create what matters. The inability to not create every day will result in being stuck in the old ways of problem-solving. Mostly when problem-solving does not work or your old way of problem-solving is blocked, you become frustrated and fail to implement a productive way to move past the problems because you only know of one way of doing things. While creating on the other hand opens new ways and exposes you to new experiences. The need to practice this approach every day is important. Learn to fill your life with thoughts of creating joy and satisfaction. Your actions and efforts will automatically start to gravitate to that state of living.

Keeping thoughts of peace, love, happiness, success, and hope will change your entire life and the structure of your brain. The neuron-plastic scientists confirm that as you think you are changing the structure of your genes, thoughts, and your whole body. Create the new you by changing your thinking. This is great news. It means you can become a new man every day. This reminds me of Lamentations, it says the Lord's mercies are new every morning and Paul says if any man be in Christ, he is a new creation. Teach this to your children, friends, and everyone around you. Well, in your own way you can create the new you without associating yourself with any religion or deity. Remember that you cannot overcome problems by trying to stop them. You can only walk in strength and release your best potentials to the best of your abilities to create a satisfying life. This can only be done when you know yourself. Know what you want.

Chapter 7 Embrace Words

Words are life; words can make you or break you — Rorisang Maimane

I enjoyed so much writing this section because every word and every sentence is proof of what you will read. Words written and shared throughout the book are evidence of the power of words. Whether the words are in song, speech, jokes, books, at the end of the day they will influence the one who receives them. Words are life, it is very sad that today we have reduced words to just communicate, nothing more. Words are more than communication. King Solomon observed this and came to conclude that, "The tongue has the power of life and death." Questions that you need to ask yourselves constantly are: Are you using words to build or destroy? Are your words filled with victory or defeat? Are you expressing words of love, blessing, compliments, thanksgiving, praise, or words of anger, hate, jealousy, and complaints? Do you desire a fruitful and victorious change in your life? Watch your words; guard your tongue, because words that go unchecked will destroy your life.

There is a powerful connection between the words you speak and your reality, be it good or bad. I encourage you to quit throwing words around like they weren't important and start using them as your life depended on it because it does. To live a life filled with prosperity and security. It is important to make sure that the words you communicate agree with what is right and true. By all means, make sure that your words agree with what you want to see manifested in your life. You simply cannot desire to prosper financially and run your mouth the whole day declaring how broke you are. When you are caught saying such negative words, you might begin to make excuses saying "but that is not what I meant". The universe is listening. What you meant will not matter so long as you do not say it exactly how you mean it. Be very careful of the conflict between what you mean to say and what you are saying. The insight of Mark tells us that, "whosoever shall say unto this mountain, be thou removed, and be thou cast into the sea; and shall not doubt in his heart, but shall believe that those things which he said shall come to pass; he shall have whatsoever he said." Take note that the words of Mark didn't say you shall have whatsoever you mean. It says you'll have what you say you want. It is what you say that counts.

The word that is spoken can never be returned or taken back. I learned that while I was still a very young man. I had a very sensitive friend during my secondary schooling years. I would say something which was very offensive. Then I would say, "I am sorry", and he would very often say that, "a word does not come back", you cannot take it back. It is true, once out, it stays out and goes to accomplish what you spoke. You must begin to say what you want to manifest in your life or prepare yourself to experience otherwise. If you desire prosperity you must say it. You must say that you are wealthy and rich beyond measures. Believe it first and then speak it.

TALK IS NOT CHEAP- TRY TO TALK WITHOUT CHOOSING YOUR WORDS AND TELL ME WHAT IS GOING TO HAPPEN

Some may think I am out of my mind, going on and on about the connection between words and your life as we know it. If I was crazy, would you on your first date perhaps run your mouth saying negative words? Try that and see what happens, that will be the first and the last time you see your date. It is the same when meeting new people, (you always want to make an impression), communicating your dreams, plans, and goals. You will choose your words carefully, why? It is important how you present yourself. Communication determines whether you will go on a second date or not. It determines whether you get the job or not. It determines whether you are understood or not, whether your goals and plans are communicated clearly. Again, try to talk without choosing your words. You will lose everything you worked for your entire life and everything you dream of building. Talk is not cheap; your talk can change your entire life.

CONFESS EVERYTHING YOU WANT, A FORM OF AFFIRMING

Do you want to be happy, get along with everyone? Do you want to flourish in everything that you do? Watch your words. Confess what you want to manifest in your life. You will soon find out what I mean by the end of this chapter. Start expressing words of respect, love, appreciation, and give thanks. It is possible to live a life without arguments and negative talks. I have experienced it and I am living it now. It was not easy at first and today I am still working on it because I am not doing it a hundred percent all the times but I am on guard of the words I speak.

You better say the right words; your life depends on the words you speak. Your words are the manifestation of your thoughts and emotions. Let me share with you a secret: have you ever wondered what people are always thinking and feeling? Well, today I am sharing with you the secret. Pay close attention to the words that people say and you will know what that person is always thinking and feeling. Every word written, spoken, or sung was first a thought and an emotion.

Words contain the power to make you or break you, this also includes your loved ones and everyone you come into contact with. Now that you know the power of your words, what is next.? As mentioned, the need to put a strong guard against your tongue is a pressing matter because you will not only be saving yourself from pain, but you will begin to shape your future. I am sure that you will enjoy building yourself up in such a way that you won't be able to contain the greatness that is growing inside of you when you put this truth into practice. If you have been worrying about things not going well for you, worrying about problems, well it is time for a change. It is time to take authority over your life by the words trapped in you. Put problems and challenges under your feet and dance on top of them, the problems will begin to worry about you. They will know not to mess with you because you have the power to destroy them.

Ever wondered why the all-powerful, mighty God used words to create everything that exists today? Wondered why God calls us to confess by using spoken words? God cherishes words; he knows the true power of words. That is why he instructs us to be reconciled with him through confessing the Lordship of his son over our lives. He knows the true power of words so much that the very earth we walk on was created by words. Why do you not take advantage of words? I encourage you to begin now.

POWER OF AFFIRMATIONS

One way I know how to use words to my advantage is by using affirmations that agree with my dreams, goals, and plans. Affirmations are the most powerful and important tools to get one step closer to your desired end results. An affirmation is a statement that one says to confirm that something is already so. Affirmations work by saying out aloud your statements, or through your mind having internal dialogues. Perhaps you may understand this as meditation.

You are using affirmations every second of your life. Your beliefs are a supporting tool for your affirmations. The internal dialogues are the most important affirmations and most dangerous if they go unchecked because they have been rooted deeply in your subconscious mind. You automatically affirm what is rooted in your mind without being fully aware that you are doing it.

For example, you might be facing a little challenge or working on a project. You have programmed your subconscious mind with discouraging and self-defeating thoughts. You automatically say that "things never go well for me". You might be telling yourself that things will not work out or saying that your situation is very bad. Under a very supervised state and full consciousness, you would not want to hear such words or think like that, but because your mind runs on autopilot, you catch yourself having negative defeating thoughts.

Your subconscious mind provides to you what you fed it for the past ten to twenty years. Such thoughts are the cause of choices you previously made, beliefs that you entertained for years. This pattern needs to change because words and thoughts that you hold in your head sum up your entire life. This will not be an easy task to do because it means that you will be reprogramming your entire mind system from scratch. You may liken this practice or process to a computer. For a computer to work to the best of its functions, software programs must be installed to run it.

Now when you are busy installing unlicensed and unauthorized software on your computer it will malfunction. Your computer will start to be slow, jam and shut down now and then. For you to make it function at its best, you must uninstall the old software, put in new licensed and authorized software. This simply means to take out the negative ideas in your subconscious mind and fill it with ideas and thoughts that will build your life.

Fill it with beliefs that you certainly chose and know will work with you for the best. Your subconscious mind does not know right or wrong, it simply accepts what your conscious mind feeds it.

When you feed your subconscious mind with negativity, pain, and discouragement it will not be able to discern the difference on its own. You need to tell it consciously. Educate your subconscious mind to run on software programs (thoughts, ideas, and internal conversations) that are clean and beneficial to your life. Monitor your thoughts and actions. Meditation and conscious choice of thoughts will be required from you constantly now more than ever.

If you are familiar with meditation you will know that it is not easy in the beginning stages but it is worth seeing it through. Meditation practices will allow you to observe your thoughts, ideas, and internal conversations. This will give you the advantage to choose your thoughts, words, and affirmations. You will begin to work on your affirmations as you see fit. Your affirmations should be specific. You can make up your affirmations by following my example. I use affirmations all the time. Very important to note is that affirmations will not work for you if you do not believe in what you are affirming. Even more important they will not work if you affirm something and go on to do differently. Some affirmations will require you to change your beliefs that have been in your mind for years.

Words are inter-connected to beliefs and thoughts. It is impossible to separate words, thoughts, and beliefs. I talked about beliefs and thoughts in chapter 5. You know that it is going to take time, as your life depends on it. It is therefore a must. Many of us long for better ways of living. You will not fill the hunger and satisfy the thirst if you are not willing to dig deeper and change some of your old ways.

The desire to succeed and to travel new roads must keep burning. Please note that your affirmations should always be in the present tense, not the future. For example, say, "I have" instead of "I will have." This gives you a sense of possessing what you already desire. That is the goal anyway, to call things that are not as they are. These acts are not a child's play or make-believe game, it is real and powerful. Your affirmations must be positive and empowering. You do not want to affirm ill will on your life by always declaring how your life is not going as good as you want it to.

You must see yourself as the best of the best because you are. You must see yourself achieving the best in everything. Your affirmations should be used to only achieve the right things, not used for selfish gains. There are good things that are not right for you so please always make sure that what you affirm is right. I learned affirmations from Louise L Hay. I recommend that you search for her written materials. I know for sure that you will receive more insight from her work. I used most of her affirmations in the beginning. Later on, I structured affirmations on my own according to my needs. Putting away debates about religion, what is true and all the arguments man loves to engage in, you will learn that the bible has some of the best affirmations to give you strength and hope.

HERE IS HOW TO AFFIRM:
I live in great abundance and prosperity
I can do all things by the power the universe has granted me
All my need are met by the universe's great abundance
I am a healthy fit person weighing 60 kg

I am more than enough to accomplish all my dreams
I accept myself for everything I am and am grateful
Today is the best day of my life because I am alive
Today is the best day of my life ever
I am grateful for all I have and I make the best out of it
Do not say what you do not want. For example, do not affirm like the following:

I do not lack anymore. Replace that with, "I live in abundance or all my needs are met."

I cannot fail. Replace that with, "I am winning."

I do not have debt, it will be, "I pay for all my needs with cash and money is flowing freely to me." I am not fat, will be, "I am a healthy, fit person weighing 60 kg" I am sure you understand.

Remember that all your affirmations should be in the present tense. Shakti Gawain also is worth checking out, he wrote a book called "Creative Visualisation" which I consider, powerfully written material and recommend that you read it. The book will give you more insight into affirmations and creative visualization.

Chapter 8 Let's Call It Sacrifice

"The world isn't all sunshine and rainbows. It's a very mean and nasty place... and I don't care how tough you are, it will beat you to your knees and keep you there permanently if you let it. You, me or nobody, is gonna hit as hard as life. But ain't about how hard you hit... It's about how hard you can get hit, and keep moving forward... how much you can take, and keep moving forward. That' s how winning is done. Now, if you know what you are worth, go out and get what you are worth. But you gotta be willing to take the hits. And not pointing fingers saying: You ain't what you wanna be because of him or her or anybody. Cowards do that and that ain't you! You're better than that" — Rocky Balboa

With the risk of assuming I will go ahead and say that many have faced deadlines before, by some miracle you managed to deliver. You fell many times but somehow you got up. You lost everything, had to start from nothing but somehow you ended up better than you were before. You have been ridiculed, excommunicated, and told that you are a failure. By some miracle you made it, you never gave up, instead, you pushed. Let me tell you, there is no miracle there. If you are looking for a miracle, that miracle is you.

You gave your best, sacrificed, and paid the price to own that medal of a winner. Can you recall a point in your life where you were pressed up against the wall? The only way out for you was to move forward by breaking through the walls to get to the other side. Can you remember the process, the energy it took, the planning, the late nights, discouragements, loneliness, the laps, practices, and setbacks? Sacrifice was in operation right there behind the scenes.

I mean you could have been somewhere enjoying the company of good friends. Perhaps sharing drinks but you chose to fight and plan. You gave your best and saw things through. Even worse you could have quit but you did not. You pressed on until victory was realised. The power of sacrifice is in you. You are the miracle, turn your hope up and start giving your best. For some of us who been privileged to be part of a sports team, playing for a major league or a school league, know very well that when it is time to get down to the ground for training sessions, that is where all the winning starts. That is where most sacrifices are made. The sacrifice I am talking about does not require slaughtering bulls and young lambs or spilling blood in any way. I am sure you can forgive me and move on if that is what your idea of sacrifice is. Here our sacrifice is something big, something magnificent that each one of us has.

During my early years of participating in athletics and soccer, I learned what it means to win before the main event begins. Something has to be offered for victory to be realised. That giving is called sacrifice; it may be the hours, efforts, and many tries and errors to perfect a skill. Also doing research or staying up till the morning working out a solution. For me, the soccer practices and the laps I did were tougher than the actual days of competing.

When other kids went playing, I had to train, making sure that I kept fit.

It was like the training was the main event and the main event was just testing my skills in front of spectators, fans, and the competition to make things more colourful. One thing I know is that if I did not get it right during practice, chances that I'd get it right during the competition were slim. I Imagine that by holding this book in your hands you have a goal; you have a dream that must come true. Whatever the dream is, by all means, it is important to give it your best. You will sacrifice something to see it done. What is it that you are willing to offer as a sacrifice to see your dream realised? Again, whatever it is that you must offer, you must keep the dream alive.

Work hard and stop for no one. It gets tough sometimes, but it gets easier, I tell you that it is worth it at the end of the day. Keep your head up. Remember that you are doing it for yourself. Remember that it is your dream and your dream alone. Sacrifice calls for a lot of personal empowerment and a lot of self-study programs whether in practice or in reading and research. Personal empowerment and development are mostly individual tasks. Yes, you will need help from time to time, but it is you who will do most of the hard work. This unfortunately will isolate you a little from your social life.

Be prepared to face loneliness especially you who are in the fields that require creativity, writing, reading, art, and very much attention to detail. I am aware that as a sketch artist I sometimes need to be around a lot of people to tap into my inspiration, but that is all there is to it. I can be around thousands but still, keep my isolation.

When your heart is filled with passion and focused on your dreams and goals, you will not miss the social life. In fact, you will not even care, so do not be alarmed. Take a chance and discover a whole new world that is waiting for you. This will require you to sacrifice something in order to access this new world. Let me say that when you are passionate and your goals are driven by love, the journey becomes less lonely and more exciting. You will face confusion, discouragement, and a lot of emotions that you may not be able to deal with. In the end, you are able to produce something magnificent when you embrace the confusion and these mixed emotions.

I am not sure exactly what you've been told, but I believe that for one to achieve greatness, in most cases one must walk alone. It is very rare for two or more people to share the same goals and passion. Take me for example, most of the time I reached out for help, communicated my dreams, plans, and goals to my friends, family and sometimes colleagues. No one cared to understand, let alone help. That's when I took it upon myself to walk the road alone. My inspiration was not shared; it was shared later when the results started showing. Many cared not about what I did; they just wanted to enjoy the end results.

Ask someone to start something big with you; they are likely to give you reasons why they cannot. Invite them to celebrate your success and share with them everything you worked hard for, see what happens. You may want to start a business, take a trip, or do something great, do not be afraid to do so even if it means doing at it alone.

The idea of working together works, yes, but not everyone will understand that burning vision that wakes you up in the middle of the night to work. No one will get your excitement when you want nothing but your space to just immerse yourself in your dream without explaining anything to anyone. Unfortunately, that is how it works. An athlete may have a coach but it is his will and his fire that keeps him going to perfect the skill. Your targets, your goal in many instances may not match with the teams or your friends because they also have their race to run.

It took me a while to understand the power of sacrifice and when I finally got a grip on that. I became quite self- assured. The results that followed the sacrifice took that assurance to the sky top. Most days I felt invincible, especially after equipping myself with the knowledge that is related to my long-term plans. Today I live my life with no regrets because I always go for what I want.

EMBRACE DISCIPLINE

It is hard to offer a sacrifice without exercising some form of discipline. Discipline is what keeps you together. It is a reminder that your offering should not go in vain when you feel like you are about to slip. Whatever you do today, whatever you will do tomorrow and whatever you will need to do ten years from now, you will never get it until you exercise some level of self-discipline. Your past achievement if you really examine and look at them, are all build within the foundation of strong discipline in some way or another.

This is one ingredient that you must master and keep close to you so long as you want to flourish. A decision to be disciplined must be a constant thing. Every man has discipline, you cannot stand anywhere as a person without discipline. The difference between a winner and a failure is that winners embrace discipline and exercise it. The act of choosing not to hang out with buddies because you have to complete an assignment is discipline.

Discipline is to commit to one goal that matters most in your life. Discipline is to know when something is not for you. Discipline is to get up in the middle of the night to study for that test or exam. The discipline to put in hours and more hours to perfect one music note, to complete a painting, a sketch, or a few chapters of a book.

In your finances, discipline is to save for your future education and to follow through on your budget plan. You also have to have the discipline to discern between a need and a want. Discipline will get you places no doubt, it is impossible to have discipline and not achieve your goals. I normally say that when your goal does not demand a deeper sense of discipline and sacrifice, then you must question your that goal.

A worthwhile goal is that which manifest the best out of you. When you are finished, you feel like you have achieved so much. Look at the performers, musicians, professional wrestlers, and athletes; these are the people who exercise the best discipline in life. I modeled my discipline by observing and learning from the commitment and discipline that musicians exercise. When they learn scales, a song or jam, they put in hours and hours until they perfect the scales. Athletes are the same. They put in the hours to keep fit and master their skills. It is not just the hours that they put into practice; it is the discipline to keep these long hours. You can do the same for yourself in any goal that you are currently working on now.

Do not use discipline when it is convenient, but use it all the time. Your ability to be disciplined in all areas of life will guarantee you tremendous success. It is being said that discipline will contribute more to your success than any other character. It was the discipline that kept me going to this day. To follow through with your plans, budget, training sessions, studying for exams you need discipline and surely a sacrifice. You cannot run away from the discipline. It is one ingredient that will serve you for the rest of your life. Napoleon Hill after interviewing over a hundred rich people came to the conclusion that self-discipline is the secret to success. Take it from me becoming disciplined is not easy. Discipline means a lot of things, but when it comes to life goals and achievements, it simply means you know your worth therefore you would do anything right to get the victory.

LET US CALL IT FAITH

In his speech" "stay hungry, stay foolish," Steve Jobs in a few words said, "Don't lose faith." These words followed right after he said, "Sometimes life hits you in the head with a brick." Now let us single out the word, "Faith." Many will listen to the likes of Steve Jobs when he talks about faith and trust, but will not listen to the teachings in the Holy book. That is the mistake that many make, instead of looking at the value of the information they judge the source of information. Move away from judging the source of information and start paying attention to the value of words communicated. Each one of us has faith in some way. You will soon understand why I say this.

Do not mistake faith for religion; if those are your thoughts right now, I urge you to stop immediately. To find out the clear and perfect understanding of faith, there must be freedom of understanding and freedom to observe without judgment and prejudices, not as Christians, Hindus, atheists, Buddhists, Pagans, or anything else. When you move past judgments you will enjoy understanding. Understanding which brings about a radical change of mind for the better. Faith is not religion or a mystery or theory; it should not be associated with any form of religion in any way. Faith is one powerful force all humans have irrespective of culture, race, and once again religion.

We all have faith as humans, we need faith to progress. Our very daily acts hang on faith. The simple dictionary meaning of faith says that faith is a complete loyalty and confidence in something. You have confidence that you passed the test, that you are successful in a job interview. You have faith that your investments will yield great returns; faith that you will make it home safe from work and that you wake up tomorrow. All that is faith. Faith is the confidence that gives you enough courage and hopes to plan for the future. Paul's letter to the Hebrews says, "faith is the substance of things hoped for, the evidence of things not seen." It is the same as the simple dictionary meaning with the difference of words that is all.

The intention is the same, believing in the things that you do not see, hoping, trusting, and knowing for a fact that, that which you want will come into your possession. You need faith to see yourself through hard times. In those hard times, you will need to draw some power and exercise faith as much as possible to fight a good fight. When you hold on until hard times pass, you are building character and instilling a sense of responsibility in you to handle the next challenge.

Your faith will turn an impossible situation into an endless series of possibilities. There will be a next challenge, some problem or crisis of some sort, you better get used to it. When your faith and trust is greater than your challenges, then you have nothing to worry about. Your marriage and friendships are purely a perfect example of faith. The fact that you are making future plans with your spouse, family, or a friend is purely an indication of faith.

Let us look at the events of Abraham and Sarah for example; putting judgments and prejudices aside. Doctors, experts would've told you that it is almost impossible for a woman to conceive after a certain age because from an age of 45 fertility has declined to a stage where it is unlikely for a woman to naturally get pregnant. In spite of all the biological factors, Abraham and Sarah managed to have a child; not one but many because of faith. Use your faith to prevail in situations that seem almost impossible. Again, Steve Jobs said you must trust that things will work out somehow, that element of having trust is faith in the end. Debates arise only when trust and faith are associated with the creator or some form of religion. Move away from such debates and focus on the truth then you will start making tremendous changes with your life. Look at your daily activities; they operate within the borders of trust and faith without you being fully aware of it.

The fact that you are able to tell someone that you will see them tomorrow is faith. You have faith that you will wake up tomorrow, that's why you tell your friends that you will meet with them tomorrow. The plans that you make when you arrange for a date after work is faith and trust. You have faith that you will make it to your date at six o'clock at that selected restaurant. It is that simple, we are beings of faith; it is in our nature. We just have different faiths. Why then is it hard for you to take up faith in all the situations in your life, especially situations that will change your life for the better? There are many things that scientists are still finding difficult to explain like the universe, how people get cured of deadly diseases and other mysteries of life. Faith is most often the answer to all of these mysteries. Take up faith and combat your life challenges. Do not try it, do it fully. You will begin to see wonders in your life. Believe that things will be alright; believe that you will win and succeed. I do not know you, but I am certain and therefore I can tell you that you can win and succeed.

Chapter 9 Eliminate Fear

*Fear is in your mind, without you, fear will not exist. —
Rorisang Maimane
"Do not let the fear of losing be greater than the excitement
of winning"— Robert Kiyosaki*

Upon deep research I discovered that many are not really defeated by change or problems, fear is the main culprit. Fear is as real as you and I; it becomes a threat no more when you get illuminated by knowledge and understanding. Fear comes when you allow it to grow by entertaining and feeding it. If left unattended, fear sticks around for so long that it takes over your whole life and then you begin to ask what could be the problem. Well, I will tell you what the problem is. It is you allowing fear to reign over your life. You give fear power without realizing it.

You are the source of fear, without you, fear cannot exist. It is very easy to see actions and decisions inspired by fear and actions and decisions inspired by faith, hope, and love. Look at man's efforts towards his dreams, goals, projects, or daily activities or when he is responsible for helping others to reach their goals. Does he go all out to give his best and make sure that everything is done right and with passion? If not, that man has fears.

Look at another man who honors appointments, meets his targets in every project, sets time aside to learn and improve his skills in the areas of his trade. He also set aside time to help and teach others to do as he does. That man is inspired by faith, hope, and love. The same man will have everything he desires because his actions are filled with faith, not fear. He believes in these efforts and makes sure that others too benefit from all his actions. He does not listen to anything that will discourage his efforts to do great things.

YOU CAN WALK ON WATER

Fear to commit to a goal, fear to confront a problem, fear of failing, fear of taking a chance, fear of the unknown, fear of getting out of the comfort zone, fear of making life-changing decisions and more importantly the fear of becoming yourself, becoming the best you can be. These are the fears that govern our day to day lives. You allow fear to pull you down; you perhaps begin to use other people or God as excuses for not living the life you deserve. Have you heard of the words, "what will people think of you?" Or do you ever say "what will people think of me if I say this and that or do this and that?" That is fear talking. Sometimes it is the fear of others talking you down. Lack of faith and trust is the reason why millions accomplish little and enjoy little. Fear becomes an unstoppable force in their lives that they miss out on opportunities presented before them. Please do not be one of them. Rise above your fears and show what you are made of.

What would you do if you could live your entire life without fear? What would you say or do if you knew that you can actually live without fear? Let us first look at the event of Peter walking on water; this is a perfect example to illustrate what fear can do to you, to your faith and trust. Peter was called to step out in faith and walk on water. At first, Peter was walking on water; he was exercising his faith living to his full potential. What then happens? Peter shifted his focus away from Christ. He looked into the waters, and he looked at the situation he was in. Fear entered when he stopped focusing on the goal. Fear asked him who are you, who are you to walk on water? You cannot do that; do you not see the stormy sea? What happened to Peter when he heard those voices in his head?

He started to sink because he shifted his focus from faith to the problem of the stormy water. I do not blame him; that is how we are taught to live in this world. We are taught to look at reality which sometimes helps, but if you want to live a life of victory you must start training yourself to live beyond reality. You are expected to see things that others do not see. Believe in the things which sound crazy to the next person. That is all there is to it.

The world we live in says what you see, is all there is. There is no room for the unthinkable, miracles, and new heights. Many out there are like Peter; are you? I trust that today you will step out in faith. Go get your dream, go create a life that you deserve. Believe in the unthinkable and eliminate your fears completely. Until you start, your fears will stick around. The only way to eradicate your fears once and for all is to go for all your dreams until everything you've ever wanted has materialized. It is very important to stay focused on the end results of your goal. Stay focused on the victory to keep your feet on the route for when fear comes. All that is outside, won't do you any good. If what you have on the inside is faith, hope, and trust then in the midst of problems everything will be OK because you are not operating by what is seen. Your internal powers, abilities, and strengths will do all the fighting for you when it seems dark.

You will not be shaken by fear, not in this lifetime. Fear has a tendency of whispering things like, "problems are bigger than your abilities, skills and your faith to get ahead." It makes you misjudge and the second question the trust you have in yourself. It makes you shift focus from the beautiful life that is great and created for you. If that sounds like you, I have great news. You can change that, take up the courage to act, and start winning in every corner. Again, it is very vital that train yourselves to believe in the unthinkable. Reality can always be changed and you have the right power to do exactly that.

The truth is that your goals and dreams are bigger than all your fears combined. Your abilities to create, holding on to the vision, and working until you see results, are all yours to make it through. Your current storms will pass; they surely will not remain in your life forever. In all the chaos there is always something to be grateful for. Make sure that you develop, grow, and have something to show when the storms pass. You can overcome anything when you decide that you will not listen to any voices except the voice that tells you that "you can." You are a winner; all things are possible and you are the best in the world. Believe in yourself, stay committed to your goals, dreams, and keep fighting until fear becomes a stranger to you.

FEAR IS LEARNED, YOU CAN UNLEARN IT AND BEGIN TO CONQUER

Fear is learned, it is not natural. I just told you the great news that fear is learned; this means it can be unlearned. Paul wrote many letters, in one of his letters to Timothy, Paul says that "we are not given the spirit of fear, but of power and of love and of a sound mind." This is great news whichever way you look at it. The words speak to each one of you to say it is your nature to be a winner; you are powerful with a very strong mind. How do you unlearn fear? It begins with the decision to stop fearing and replacing the fear with the higher powers of creativity, vision, purpose, affirmations, and love. All these powers make fear nothing.

See victory, see the courageous and brave you, facing life's challenges with an unstoppable power of knowing that come what may, your situation is only temporary; what matters most is the life you want to create. Use all the resources you have to build your life as you see fit. It is the goal of the creator to see you prosper in everything. Keep clean and victorious thoughts, this is one powerful way to help you eliminate all fears. Keeping positive thoughts alone will not help you if you do not take action towards creating the life you want.

This simply means that action will be one massive key antidote to fear. When you confront your fears, you are acting. When fear comes creeping along in the dark you must know that you have the spirit of power, love, and a sound mind. You must also ask what actions you should take to eliminate fear. What are you really afraid of? Answer these questions and then begin to take massive action. Look to yourself for strength. Search deeper, meditate, and call out all the Universal forces to back you up. Build up your abilities and strength by connecting with the higher power and then your fears will not bother you any longer.

Marianne Williamson in her book: A Return to Love Wrote:
... "Our deepest fear is not that we are inadequate. Our deepest fear is that we are powerful beyond measure. It is our light, not our darkness, that most frightens us. We ask ourselves, who am I to be brilliant, gorgeous, talented and fabulous? Actually, who are you not to be? You are a child of God. You're playing small doesn't serve the world. We were born to make manifest the glory of God that is within us. It's not just in some of us; it's in everyone. And as we let our own light shine, we unconsciously give another people permission to do the same. As we are liberated from our own fear, our presence automatically liberates others.

Chapter 10 Embrace knowledge

"Education is the most powerful weapon which you can use to change the world"— Nelson Mandela

Your challenges, struggles, and suffering will not go away unless you understand their root cause. Most of the time we think that end results or consequences of the challenge are the problems, sadly that is not so. For example, when you are struggling with debt or financial lack, it is very easy to mistakenly think that debt or lack of financial resources is the real problem. You overlook your actions, spending habits, your emotions, psychology, beliefs about money, and also your lack of planning and action to generate income. Debt is only the end result of something you are not doing right with your finances. It could be that you do not budget, or you live above your means. You buy with emotions, using shopping as an escape from dealing with the reality of your stressful events or you are simply irresponsible and clueless. Examples are many; look at people who struggle with gaining too much weight, the problem is not the food they eat.

It is not that they do not exercise; it is often their desire to eat everything they crave and everything that looks good. The problem of health risk due to smoking and drinking is rooted in something else. The problem is not that you smoke and drink, the problem is what drives you to do it in the first place. Why do you do it? Why do you have that desire to smoke and drink? Deal and control your inner desires and then most of the life struggles will be gone forever. The problem is that the inner desires lead people astray if not controlled.

Dealing with the root cause is different from dealing with the actions. You cannot deal with the root cause if you have no knowledge and understanding of your problem. Only knowledge can save you from all your struggles. Your goals and dreams fail because you do not invest in knowledge. Every failure we have experienced is because of disobedience to principles and our ignorance to knowledge. We try our level best to come up with solutions to solve the problems before us. We love quick fixes. Very often the solutions that we come up with are not permanent.

They are just temporary reliefs until the problems come creeping back again. See, it is like this; when you have a headache caused by worrying too much. This leads to a lack of sleep and eventually body pains and extreme exhaustion. You would take aspirin or perhaps pain killers to get rid of the headache. The headache will stop at that time. The trick is that aspirin is not giving you a permanent solution to your headache. It is only giving you a relief to get by another hour or day without that headache. Tomorrow the same headache is back again.

What you do is that you take another aspirin because it seemed to work yesterday. You get caught up in a never-ending circle. You have not dealt with the source of the headache. In this way, you are only dealing with the symptoms. What will happen after some time is that your head will start feeling heavy and painful again. You overlooked the real problem, which caused you to worry. Find the cause of your worry and restlessness and you will have the answer to solve your headache.

The only way out for you is to deal with the cause. For you to get to the cause you need to dig deeper with patience, get the knowledge and understanding. This process of digging deeper for the real cause of problems is long but it is worth it. Not only do you find solutions to problems, but you discover how you can prevent problems of the same nature from happening in the near future. Ever heard that prevention is better than cure? This approach is giving you exactly that, saving you from making the same mistake again.

VICTORY BEGINS FROM THE INSIDE

First win the battle inside, then outside will be a walk in the park. Your desires to eat too much, to drink, and to smoke are internal. We cannot see them but that is where the problems are. Eliminate the things which cannot be seen, and then the visible will be easy to eliminate. That is why we hear that the big fight is first in the mind. That is your fears, doubts, insecurities, bad habits, lack of confidence, and worries.

Everywhere you go, you will notice that people are very busy working tirelessly to improve their circumstances. They, therefore, have the desire to improve. This is true for each one of us. We want to improve our finances, work on our marriages, relationships lives, and achieve our long-term goals and plans. We want to look beautiful by going to the gym. We want to climb the corporate ladder and feel that we achieved. It will be impossible for you to improve and achieve all these desires when you are not willing to improve yourself.

A good place to start is with learning, getting knowledge and understanding, then applying what you have learned. We confuse ourselves; give ourselves unnecessary stress in trying new ventures without learning and understanding. We frustrate others by getting into relationships with them without first having the knowledge of how to treat another human being better.

We confuse ourselves so much with so many things without understanding why. We are looking in the wrong direction. We start to improve our lives when we know and understand that the first thing to improve is you, your thoughts and actions. Instead of merely trying too hard to change your financial status, poor relationships, businesses that are failing, goals and dreams that are not being realised, or our social state, we need to do things differently by watching our thoughts and behaviours. This process will provide you with insight to do things better with every next try. That is all there is to it. It is that simple, knowledge first, then the rest will follow. If you alter your thoughts, feelings, and behavior about the problems, the battle is halfway won.

Problems do not think; you are a thinking being. You give your circumstances power over you when you do not understand them. You can take that power back by means of understanding. When you have knowledge and understanding of your circumstances, you will begin to direct and utilize your thoughts, feelings, and actions towards the direction that is beneficial to you. Getting to know why you encounter a problem after problem is a good move to make starting from today.

Have you ever heard the saying, "use your pain for good or turn lemons into lemonades?" I am sure you have. That's what we are going to do here, turn our difficulties into successful learning opportunities. That is what I did with debt; I used debt to gain financial freedom. You cannot gain such an advantage if you are misinformed or lacking knowledge. You can only do that through education and knowledge. First, know what you are dealing with and why you are in that situation in the first place. Do not wait for tomorrow but start empowering yourself now. Take note that you are the most intelligent creation in the world. Our ancestors came from far to give us powerful methods to make our lives better. They used knowledge to build the world we live in today.

Take advantage of that to build the life you want to live. Problems do not think, speak, and make decisions, you, on the other hand, you can think, speak, and make decisions.
Use such simple gifts to your advantage. Struggle not, because you already have the upper hand. Take advantage of your problems and become a better person once and for all. I did it. King Solomon in Ecclesiastes wrote that nothing is new under the sun. Nothing in this world is new. This tells you that everything you are going through right now or everything that you will go through in life someone somewhere has already faced it. This is good news because it means that there is a book, a written material, podcast, video, or something out there for you to get your hands on for the purpose of learning to overcome any of your struggles.

I would recommend for everyone to read every day, not because it is fun, (well it is fun for me) but because your life depends on it. For all the problems in the world, there is a solution in a book somewhere. You just have to find it. Books solve problems all the time. You do not have to read all books, choose books related to your area of need and stop reading a book called, "Facebook".

Do you want to be successful and have the best of everything in life? Then start reading, read about our leaders and great people who are successful today. If the richest man in the world today read 50 books and more a year, why not you? You might be embarrassed to know that the reason why you struggle so much is that you do not want to read and empower yourself. If only you knew that picking up a book will boost your thinking and change your life completely you would make it a habit. Start reading today, young people; you will be amazed by how much knowledge can transform your lives. In my case, I found a lot of written material on debt and finances. I found videos on YouTube and I sought help from professionals.

I suggest you go to your library, go to your internet, and buy your newspaper, magazines related to your area of interest. Find out who has been in the same circumstances you are in and then learn from them. Find out how they did it. Read and educate yourself, be better than yesterday. I want to close off this chapter by highlighting some truths. Number one is that prayer without action will not change the circumstance in your life - be it unhealthy marriage, relationships, lack of money, and more. You simply need to pair your prayers with action - digging for knowledge and then acting on it. No amount of prayer and wishing will substitute the importance of hard work and action.

You will say prayer does not work when it is you who does not work. I believe that it will benefit us a great deal to work on increasing our knowledge every day. As mentioned, no amount of prayer can substitute the importance of knowledge and taking action. Prayer will not magically put ideas in your head. You must first seek the knowledge and then ideas will be generated by what you have learned. No matter how much you pray your problems won't go away, your circumstances will not change and you will not reach your goals if you do not seek knowledge and act on it.

It might sound more like an instruction; trust me it is not my intention to do so. However, I have to emphasise the need for befriending knowledge. Learn as much as you can, get knowledge, and develop some skills. Put plans in order then make sure you follow through with your plans. Imagine this, we have two gardeners, both have the same goal which is to have plenty of vegetables filling their gardens. One man purchases a piece of land then get s on his knees to pray for harvest and the other after purchasing land, carefully begins to plan, learn of all the methods of gardening vegetables, call out for help from others to help him work his garden. Would you not say that the second man is wise and deserves to enjoy the fruits of his labour? The same example applies to all circumstances in your life. When you plan, work, and do more work, you can turn every circumstance to yield your desired end results. If you're like the first gardener, you will certainly wait forever to enjoy the fruits of your 'labour'. All these begin with knowledge.

GET KNOWLEDGE OR PAY THE PRICE

"My people are destroyed for lack of knowledge," Hosea could not have said it any better. The opening quote should be written somewhere in the sky with big letters for all to see. The words that Hosea wrote are very important, for I have seen many falls because of a lack of knowledge. I have fallen too. Nelson Mandela understood the importance of the knowledge that is why he said education is the most powerful weapon which you can use to change the world. James Allen beautifully captured the importance of knowledge with the following words, "Looking out upon the world, we behold it as an arena of strife in which individuals, communities, and nations are constantly engaged in the struggle, striving with each other for superiority, and for the largest share of worldly possessions". As much as many are destroyed because of a lack of knowledge, I believe that there is more than meets the eye.

Consider this for a moment: our leaders are educated. They have degrees from the best universities in the world; some even know the word of God. They counsel with the wise - leaders equally intelligent as they are, but it is these same leaders that sometimes destroy our societies, blocking opportunities for the destitute.

We look to our leaders for guidance and leadership but their acts are filled with corruption, selfishness, the pursuit of power, and fires of passions to satisfy their needs. More often than not our leaders know what is right; why then are they not doing the right thing? Please do not assume that when I say our leaders, I refer to heads of the states and religious leaders alone. Every individual is a leader in their respective environment. You are a leader in your home, at work, in the sports ground, in your marriage, at school, at church, and in the business world. Everywhere there are leaders.

We are all connected; the small actions that one individual does have the potential to pollute or enrich the entire world. Your failure to be a good leader makes others pay the price, not a good price if I may say.

You and I cannot change what we do not know, that is why the first step is getting knowledge and understanding. I shared with you the nature of problems; remember I said that problems can be used as an advantage and surpassed by greater acts. Let us explore some causes of the problems we mostly have in life. Problems are not just personal; they extend to our neighbours, friends societies, nations, and then to the far ends of the world. I do not claim to have an ability to solve the world's problems; I do not know what the rest of the world is going through. What I do know is that there is no problem big enough or impossible to overcome.

I will reveal some simple causes that stir up strife and problems in our lives. The world of problems cannot exist without man; man, therefore, is the number one source of problems. Imagine you are sitting at home reading your favourite book or making breakfast for your family and you hear on the news that a nearby town has been bombed. What do you do? You panic thinking that maybe your town is next? You could be right, you could be wrong, but above all that, the question that comes to mind is who? The "who" is asking of someone - who could have done such and why? The answer is that it was a person; a human being caused such distress which is leading you to panic.

Learn about the cause of some of your problems and then you will begin to work towards improving that particular area of course. Through my research, I discovered many causes of common human distractions. I however believe that all chaos and distractions boil down to one being, man. Man is the primary source of problems. Let's connect everything together to make sense of what I am speaking of. Ignorance is a powerful foe that destroys many. In ignorance, a man brings to himself pain and suffering, which then consumes and destroys him. Ignorance lurk where selfish desires and passions, and laziness lurk.

You can break it down, observe it from individuals, families, religions, nations and then spread it worldwide. At some level somewhere we become ignorant. At the very same time, we know what is right and choose to do otherwise, that is why we always pay the price in pain and suffering. Is it ignorance or disobedience? It is both truly. Those that are learned, especially our leaders, know what is right but often choose to disobey righteousness. Laws are set in place to protect us but somehow someone chooses to live above those laws. No matter how small the disobedience is, someone ends up paying with painfully.

I can generally say that ignorance and lack of caring are rife, but I am sure that many are doing the right things and trying their level best to do well. Social movements are formed every day around the world. There are people standing up for human rights, protection of animals, and preserving natural resources. Why? Because somehow, something is not done right. There would not be any movements if things were done right. We cause more harm than we ever could imagine. Organisations are teaching many to be employees instead of employers, innovators, business owners, depriving many to use their mental abilities to the best of their potentials. Education systems teach kids to add one plus one without telling them why. All is done in the name of progress, claiming that it is necessary; but is it really necessary?

As I have mentioned, we are not taught to deal with problems and changes that challenge a human being to fulfill his purpose in life. These are the societies we live in, where intelligence and success are measured by how well you scored against others; how better you are by owning all expensive materials, and how much money you have. Values, purpose, relevant knowledge, peace, love, and care, are left out in the daily agenda by our leaders and the societies. Instead of helping one another we compete and oppress.

Competition is deeply rooted in our minds. Becoming better is not about you becoming better, it is becoming better than the next person. So long as I am better than you, we then can get along. If you are better than me, we cannot get along. There is always a division. You will soon learn how this affects you as an individual to flourish and create the successful life you deserve. Man's entire life is based on thinking, instead of teaching thinking.

The system is teaching you to follow and compete to climb the corporate ladder. To self-indulge, have power and control all the world's resources (oil, diamonds, lands). All these are deeply rooted in the heart of man's desire to gain dominion over all things. Power drives us to corrupt even the smallest things in our lives which result in individuals suffering, having difficulties and frustrations in every corner. Unconventional thinking is totally ignored.

Myles Munroe in his book the kingdom principles says that "The greatest threat to civil society is mankind. Every day the flood of images on our television screens tells the sad story. Blood, death, diplomacy, conflict, hatred, fear, poverty, starvation, rape, genocide, refugees and human migration, natural disasters, daily bombings, economic uncertainty, immigration, corporate corruption, moral decay, the sexual revolution, and the clash of counter cultures- all of these testify to the undeniable fact that we are our own worst enemy." This observation can be reduced to three things, ignorance, selfishness, and lack of knowledge. All the bad things that are happening are just but a product of selfishness and truly, the absence of knowledge to do what is right. It is the desire of man to always want more than what he already has; on many occasions at the expense of others. That is why there are bombings, attacks, and serious declines in our economies. When men realise that the universe has more than enough for everyone to live and share, individuals, begin to succeed on a personal level because nobody is fighting you and trying to stop you from becoming the best you can be.

Man will come out of the darkness and into the light. Knowledge will befriend him and from there onwards he will seek to deal with all things under the sun justly. He will seek opportunities where no strife will ever arise. He will not impose his will on others. Upon such acts and realisation, a man will be satisfied and have peace. The very act of eradicating ignorance out of our hearts is the beginning of a satisfying life filled with love and hope. Man must come to terms with the fact that he needs God, not religion, to lead a happy and successful life. He needs to add value and fulfill his purpose not to accumulate things. You might ask and wonder how is this all connected to you and the flourishing lifestyle

One - You need knowledge and leadership skills to be successful. Without good leaders and knowledge, your efforts to flourish will be difficult.

Two - You will need all the resources you can get to succeed; you cannot utilize resources at their best if your nations, society, and economy are in shambles. Three - Where there are selfishness and domination, it is safe to say that there is no peace. Without peace, you as an individual cannot be at your best to fulfil your purpose or to flourish.

Chances are that you constantly worry and are always fighting unfruitful battles. The above diagram sets a picture in your head of how we are all connected. A nation, a good nation is led by good knowledgeable leaders who care and have your best interest at heart. When a nation flourishes, families and its society flourish as well. This great life is empowered by individuals who work together to do only great things. You simply cannot argue that such environments will produce nothing but successful and satisfied people. It all goes back to knowledge and the ability to put such great knowledge to better use. You are very important; you have a role to play in the large world.

Chapter 11 Embracing Change

Look at the times' oh child of earth; do we not have night then followed by a day or have a day then followed by night? Do we not have sunshine when we awake then later have noon? Do we not have winter which later gives way for spring, summer, and autumn? Do we not cheer, sing and dance some days and then some days mourn?

Were we not told that in all things there are seasons? Time to sow and time to reap? Time to be born and time to die? Then why the despair when happy circumstances give way for a time of chastening? Why cry "oh why me" "oh why is this happening to me"? Are you not yet learned in the school of wisdom? Have you not seen that it is the order life to let go of the old and give way to the new? Do you say that the night is as not useful as the day? Listen I am telling you that both night and day are as much use to him who is rooted with purpose and vision.

The heart with purpose knows how to divide his efforts to both night and day. Both night and day are profitable to him

who is a good steward. Can you show me one mortal who is not subject to the changing of ways or who is not to be tried for the purpose of faith, growth, and obedience?
Why cry? Be strong, learn to know that which is good for you for, change is good for you. Let go of foolish dreams thinking that life will always be sweet and roses. Time to be humbled is permitted and therefore it should be welcomed with arms open wide. A soul that is destined for success will know and expect a change in circumstances, he will prepare and flourish in both time of sowing and reaping. For in sowing also there is harvest. The very act of sowing with purpose and a goal at heart is a victory on its own.
It is good for you to stay committed to your best efforts and services in all changes. Every minute has its own purpose, you might now know why but rest assured that your efforts and commitments will not go unrewarded. Have little sense of patience and while waiting equip yourself with knowledge and understand oh child of earth, for in doing so you will be like a tree that will survive all kinds of a season and still produce many fruits.

NATURE OF CHANGE

Change is one of the best things that ever happen to humanity. The processes of creating will always bring forth fruits and fulfilling of benefits. While you are busy solving problems, someone is appreciating life. "Life is changing. Work is changing. Families are changing. The economy is changing. The climate is changing. Even the rate of change is changing. Many feel like they're at the mercy of circumstances. Buffeted by change, they are unable to cope with what life throws at them.

Only a few have what it takes to meet the challenges. The majority, thinking that what they want is not possible, settle for what they have. Others quit. Stuck, stalled, drifting, they fail to create what they care about. Many escapes into ruts and routines and waste their time on tv, overeating, Facebook, Twitter and video games, alcohol, and other drugs. These fixes are temporary. Often the cure is worse than the disease.

We are not taught to welcome, access, and manage change. The idea of welcoming change is not very common. We want things to always be the same. We hear people say, "he or she changed," "so-and-so is not the same person I married." You should be happy that they changed. For nothing can progress or become a success without going through change. The frightening thing you can experience is living with someone who does not change or circumstances that do not change.

Change is always good unless your mind tells you otherwise. In this life "no change" means being stuck and not moving in any direction. That is not good. Responding to change positively to add to our benefits does not come naturally. It is our responsibility to make an effort to learn and then move on. These are the best approaches to respond to change. Marcus Aurelius spoke about change beautifully in his meditations, he said: "Observe constantly that all things take place by change, and accustom thyself to consider that the nature of the Universe loves nothing so much as to change the things which are, and to make new things like them."

Change present options to you, you can either respond or react. If you choose to do nothing, alas, the harm will be done to none but you. You will eventually do something; why not begin to do it now? Moving forward, because you were not taught to deal with change, how do you know which approach is best for you? Let us explore briefly what could be the best option for you.

REACTING TO CHANGE

Reacting to change simply means when change happens, you are always on the defensive. It finds you unprepared and you feel inconvenienced. You can pick up by now that this is not a good and right way to handle change. Reacting to change is mostly motivated by fear, worry, and uncertainty. People who live in fear of uncertainty usually do not plan, even if they plan, they do not trust in their plan and worse they do not expect the best out of life. Many instead of standing up when change comes, they start by resisting change they try to fight it to keep things the same to suit their comfort. They will always look for excuses to avoid engaging with the changing times. Such people watch change happen. They talk and criticize people who welcome change.

If you are in any of the above-mentioned situations it is time to switch gears and look at the change in a more constructive way. You deny yourself many opportunities by resisting change. Shying away from seizing the opportunity, to take the lessons of reality can be much of a higher price to pay in the end. I know this since I have ignored the change in my finances many times. I have ignored the signs when life called out to me for growth. When financial armageddon hit me, at first, I denied it, thinking that I am doing alright until one day I woke up feeling the weight. By that time, I was already in too deep, I had two credit cards which owed a minimum of r15 000 each, I had an overdraft of r20 000 and few store cards which rounded up to R5 000. I barely kept up with the minimum monthly instalments.

Whenever I paid my monthly instalment, I'd end up with nothing for myself to live on. This happened because I ignored changes in my finances and lifestyle. I resisted change and continued to live like I have money when I did not. I denied the fact that I lived way above my means. This led me to worse situations. Surely upon deep research, lots of planning, and hard work I ended up breaking free from the bonds of financial misfortunes. This came about when I first accepted that I needed help. This was also the acceptance of the change. Instead of reacting, I started responding with proper planning as mentioned. First, I made learning a habit. I found out all I could about debts, savings, and financial investments, debt. I established my business and worked my way up until I achieved my goals.

RESPONDING TO CHANGE

Following up on the last topic of reacting to change, this then leads us to the winners, people who make change happen. These are the people who respond to change. Even better these are people who initiate change when they see fit. If I were you, I would make a decision right now to fall into this category. Winners plan, prepare, and follow through with their plans. They fully understand the principles and truth about change. They embrace change. Initiating and responding to change means you know better. You understand and are ready to give your best. This means you have prepared accordingly. It starts with accepting the fact that change is going to happen irrespective of what you may want or feel.

This goes deeper than just accepting; it is a matter of knowing that this life is created in such a way that there will always be a change in seasons. All seasons have great benefits for all who are able to recognize the benefits. Everyone knows that winter is coming, you cannot be surprised by winter, and if you are surprised by winter then surely you need help. You can prepare for winter by buying warm clothes. While you shop for winter you know in the back of your mind that winter will not last. Again, you prepare for spring as much as you did for winter. It is the way of life; you cannot say 'but I did not know'. it is just the same with your finances and your life, you have to prepare for the future.

You may put policies and investment plans in place for children to go to school. Before children are born, you sometimes purchase clothing, toys, prepare their room, and other necessities. Your car has a spare wheel in case of a flat tyre. You prepare for an interview, plan for your goals, and so on. Life is about preparations and making the necessary adjustments when change happens. There is no room for complaints. When change comes, all your preparations will give you a good start by acting with confidence instead of reacting with fear.

All the above examples of preparing will give you peace. Surely you will rest well at night when you know you have prepared very well. This paves a way for yourself to plan and work on other things. With preparations in order you are never surprised nor fearful when the unexpected happens. Preparation in the spirit by engaging with the ways of the spirit is primary to all preparations. When the preparation of the spirit is covered, preparation of the mind, emotions, and the physical become easier.

In a way, I am saying, prepare the inner man first, and then the others will follow. Winners enjoy benefits of change because they prepare themselves spiritually, mentally, and physically. They also take pride in initiating change that benefits others around them. They know how to prepare for the future. Their families never lack for they have the ability to make changes in their finances, career, and business. Are you a winner who knows how to prepare for change? If not please do not despair, this book will teach you exactly how to prepare yourself for any change that might come.

HAVE EYES FOR A CHANGE

Change, when rightly perceived becomes one of the best keys to progress. Something must change for progress to happen. For your body to receive energy and grow strong, the food you ate needs to go through the process of change to provide nutrients to your body. For a tree to develop into a full tree, it goes through the process of change. Change influences many of your days to day operations.

Just because you do not notice it happening around you, it does not cancel its operation and existence. For example, small changes like trees growing, this means that the temperature of the air and soil starts to warm up and the hours of daylight increase as the days get longer. You get to enjoy spring and of course summer. You will get to experience two types of changes, change imposed, and change by choice. The latter is the sweetest. Both of them hold high potential for learning.

Change by choice is very much handled positively with ease. Imposed change hits you the most unexpected times. How you respond to changes imposed and change by choice has a much great influence on your entire life. Everything around you operates through the laws of change. The weather, evolution, health, and success, all these are subject to change. You yourself are a good example of change, your body and your entire being changes every day. That is why the author of Ecclesiastes says that everything has its time and season.

The author knew that changes must take place for things to progress.

Change in a form of difficulties may reveal characters and personalities that surprise everyone around you, yourselves included. Sometimes you surprise yourself with your strength and abilities to handle difficult matters. Until change takes place, until difficulties come to you, you may never fully understand your strength and your capacity to overcome such difficult times. That is why it is important to prepare. Preparations should be in order for you to respond to change effectively. Preparations of the mind, finances, and physical, emotional should be in place. Prepare for what you desire to take place in your life and also prepare for the unknown. The planning and preparations put your life at ease. It takes away the worries and fear of the unknown. Preparation is like taking insurance. Only this time you have full control of how your insurance pays off. When you are ready, mentally, physically, and emotionally you will be like a tree planted with its roots reaching deep down in the core of the earth. Come storms, come rain you will be immovable. You will be strongly rooted and confident of the future.

COMFORT, THE ENEMY OF CHANGE

Comfort is the biggest enemy of change. Comfort and good times can turn things into norms, traditions, and routines. The founder of the House of Kayise, Melody Mazibuko said that "familiarity tends to breed contempt and that any work routine eventually starts to become a bore and demotivating when repeated over a thousand times". Do not find yourself in that state. You should be careful not to get very comfortable, if things are not changing you must seek and initiate change yourself, it is one way of creating joy and fulfillment.

When dealing with change your body and mind might take some time to accept the changes. The good news is you can change. You can simply do so by constantly making a decision to change. When you begin to understand and embrace change you will notice that it comes in different ways. The change that happens within us, change that happens around us, change that happens to us, and the change that we make. This is great news. This means that you have a choice. You have some form of control in all the four changes. That is why I am so excited and embrace what happens around me. I am sure you also heard that change produces different types of people. Those who watch the change, who make a change, and who talk about change. Which one are you?

BENEFITS FROM CHANGE

Change allows us time to sow and then later allow us to enjoy the harvest. Every new morning comes bearing new beginnings, change does the same. It gives opportunities to create new things, new habits, thoughts, and actions. It allows us to let go of the old. If you are not happy with your current state, you may simply seize that opportune moment to change. You can make that decision now and see your life flourish.

With change by your side, it is very much guaranteed that all your current struggles will not last. As mentioned, there is time for everything. All things change every day and surely some events in your life will change dramatically and unexpectedly. Tragedy, illness, and death of a loved one or someone close may force you to try to rearrange your life in ways you never thought possible. Somehow day by day all the pieces fall in place, and you will find the new normal. I was once forced to deal with change in the most uncomfortable way possible, in 2015 I was involved in a car accident. Thankfully I did not suffer any physical injuries but I was left with many challenges. I was faced with the decision to fix the car or buy a new one. I had to adjust, pay this and that. There were so many things going on in my head. In any case, I was not prepared for all of that. You can imagine also the readjustments that I had to make. Going back to use public transport and all the inconvenience I had to deal with compared with the comfort of having your own private transport.

It was not that frightening when I finally started to come to my senses. When I began to deal with this change in a more responsive way, I started to learn many new things about cars. I became a more careful and better drive. The benefits did not end there. I started appreciating more. I was humbled, learned that all material things come and go, hence today I never get attached to materials.

James Allen says that a man who identifies himself with his possessions will feel like all is lost when all his possessions are gone. I understand what that really means. Going back to the benefits of my change, I built new relationships, got to understand how insurance companies operate. More importantly, I learned to prepare for the worst. The change did not look so much of a benefit at first because reality was, I am in an accident and that is all I saw in front of me. As much as I am trying to allow you to look at the change in a good way, it is not always an easy thing to do. It takes time but it is very much possible. When you finally grab that lesson, I promise you are never the same person.

When things are done right with understanding you will find yourself way much happier and successful than you could ever have been. This is what happened to me after the car accident. It is also what happened to Job. He lost everything for the purpose of gaining ten times more. Your life could be in the stage where you see more loss than gains. When your reality is frightening in some way, do not worry. Change will ensure that all your worries and your fears do not last. You will rise once again. Change will deliver solutions and great success to you. When such events take place, you need not grieve and despair. Any day of your life can be the best day of them all, could be the beginning of your best years. You can direct that by taking small positive steps toward any desired end results. Today can be your new normal, how do you want to begin your new normal?

I am going to close off this chapter the words of Marcus Aurelius;

We shrink from change; yet is there anything that can come into being without it? What does Nature hold dearer, or more proper to herself? Could you have a hot bath unless firewood underwent some change? Could you be nourished if the food suffered no change? Is it possible for any useful thing to be achieved without change? Do you not see, then, that change in yourself is of the same order, and no less necessary to Nature?

– Marcus Aurelius, Meditations 7:18

Chapter 12 Change Manifest Value

"Everything of value must go through the process of change."
— Rorisang Maimane

When change comes, it makes us question our lives. It becomes almost impossible to not begin to wonder whether you are adding value to your life and the lives around you. Perhaps some do not think about what value they add but I do. I had asked a friend if he thinks his life was adding value. My friend told me that he hears and understands very well what I am asking him. He said, "I rather not think about it." He went on to say, "your question of value leads to the question of purpose and many of life's challenging questions, and like many people I choose to suppress such thoughtful questions. They are not easy to deal with especially when society has taught us to be slaves to trends. I rather think about what I am going to do and how I am going to do it to make my next few thousand rands," he said.

I did not question my friend further, I just sat there quietly but my mind was so loud, I could hear voices in my head saying there is another way. Somehow, I deeply understood what he meant. I myself have felt like that. What was important to me was to pick up my next pay-check and put food on the table, nothing more. You might want to think about that for a moment, maybe not in a general sense as I put it, but more on a deeper level because we are talking about your life. Ask more questions; question your actions and day to day efforts. Is this worth doing? Does this bring me value? What is value? Why do I do what I do? How does it add value? What do I value to me? I cannot answer those questions for you but I can give you something to start with.

Man sacrifices his character, good judgments, and righteousness for material things. Solomon's marvellously rich expression indicates that man will do wrong for a piece of bread. In another translation, he says, "But some judges will do wrong to get even the smallest bribe." What do you sacrifice your time, character, and good judgments for? I believe that you sacrifice your time, character, and virtues because it is valuable to you. Your life is measured by the time you have and the virtues you build in your given time. Man always sacrifices that which he believes to be lesser in favour of that which he believes to be greater. It took me eight years to finally understand half of the things I value, why I value them, and what I was willing to do to get them. Today the questions of value-adding life are still circling in my mind.

YOUR JOURNEY TO SELF-DISCOVERY BEGINS WITH VALUE

"Try not to become a man of success, but rather try to become a man of value" — Albert Einstein

When I ascended to a level where money and possessions were nothing but a fraction in living a fulfilling life, I began to seek for things of value. I cherished time, love, knowledge, and friendship more. I started to create what mattered to me. Something magnificent happened to me, I started seeing people differently, I began to understand individuals and love them more for their differences. My conversations started to take a different form; I changed the books I read to books that talk directly to my new way of living. You can imagine making a decision like that came with its packages.

The temptation to give up, telling myself to quit this new path, and to go back to my old life was the easy way out. Good for me, I never gave up. I had hope, faith, and strength in my spirit to keep myself from wandering off course. Therefore, my spirit was greater than the temptation. My desperate need to do better was always great, it is always my guide. I never let a day pass by without creating what matters to me, this then leads to a very good way to give back to those who are willing to receive.

I began to work on enjoyable projects, I read and wrote more. I immersed myself in research web development and created more art. I reactivated my childhood desires to learn music and casually stirred hope and inspiration in the hearts of those who wanted to receive it. I spoke with the boldness that gained me favour with people. Relationships changed; I became alive for the first time. I turned every rock to pursue my purpose the reason I am living, breathing, and burning energy. I learned that I was not on this earth to solve problems, have money, live luxuriously, and then die, of course. I rather enjoy living in privilege now and then but there is always more. I am here to put something in this world. I am here to touch and change lives, to add value and give hope to others. I am here to fight for someone who cannot do the fighting for themselves at that given time and I choose to be the light of the world.

Building character and discipline was easy when I discovered that I should strive for value. My steps and direction were guided and disciplined by my goals and dreams. I did not need to please or entertain anyone at the cost of my time. Things like clubs, parties, sex, women, alcohol, and hanging out for the sake of hanging out did not excite me anymore. I was on a journey to becoming what I am today, a great man a man of value. Life became much simpler because the things that did not excite me any longer where mostly the source of my headache. Like the need to feel important and to impress. In my way, I am saying that I found a way to a valuable life. It could be different for you of course. Ask yourself this also, could what you are doing now be the reason you are not at peace and some of your best endeavours fail? You might do other things that are different from mine and somebody else's but do keep the value-adding system as a guide.

There are many paths to lead a valuable life. You may not like what I do or like, that is in fact much better and OK because your uniqueness is what the world needs. The world responds better when you use your unique gifts to make everything better and beautiful. In that way, you will add value. Value is the impact you make to the world; the influence you make to create better lives for everyone around you.

Every human has a need to be valued, but the expression of the need to be valued varies with individuals. Whoever you are, you know deep down that you have that one thing (if not many) that gives your life a sense of greater value. Many of us are misled by the race for material possessions and the appearance of what seems valuable. We chase after things hoping to fill the need to be of value and lead important lives.

THERE IS NO VALUE IN POSSESSIONS, ONLY DISAPPOINTMENTS

"A man's life does not consist in the abundance of his possessions." — *Luke*

Putting value on possessions is a sure way to greater disappointments. I learned that from personal experience that nothing possessed materially guarantees you happiness, peace, love, and value. When you lose your possessions, what happens then? It will mean that your value, peace, and joy are lost because your possessions became the center of your value system. Certainly, you do not want that.

Things get lost, damaged, and stop serving their intended purposes. Where does that leave you? Does it mean you stop living, being happy, and lose value? That is why it is important to learn the true nature of what is valuable. That's why you must place value on eternal things. Mathew spoke about the treasures in heaven that cannot be stolen and cannot lose value. These treasures are not some mysterious things that only a chosen few can achieve; No. These treasures are actually in you already, waiting for you to make an effort to uncover them. Try to put aside theories and debates and think about the importance of what Matthew is trying to make you see and understand. Think about having something of value that is yours and yours alone which cannot be lost or stolen. When you implement that way of thinking, you will begin to want to use your efforts only on what matters, on the things of value.

Knowledge, talents, abilities, and specializing in certain sets of skills are your treasures and a big difference-maker in your life. When you understand this, the life of value is easy. You have so many powerful forces inside of you that not even a human mind can come to comprehend. You are amazing; you are special and gifted in all possible ways. Work on your unique gifts and skills. That is how you add value to your life. Money, clothing, cars, and other luxuries you chase, are lifeless burdens that lead to a lot of worries and frustrations. Having all this becomes a problem to maintain.

It is very easy to fantasize about owning beautiful luxurious cars or big homes, however in that fantasy one does not usually think about cleaning the car, fixing and repairing this and that and so on. I understand. I mean who would want to think about cleaning and repairing. You just want to enjoy your material gains, the drudgery tasks that follow are something you do not want to deal with. How then do you protect that which is here and gone tomorrow?

The car that you are driving may have insurance protection, but it can still catch fire, breakdown, rust, and get stolen or damaged in some way. Cell phones are dropped daily, clothing fits you today, and tomorrow they do not. Money is here and then gone the next day. Do not get me wrong the above should be enjoyed; they are purely harmless when you do not obsess over or idolize them. I also do not mean to sound negative or scare you. My intention is to entice thoughts of focus towards creating value and adding it. I want you to consider deeply what is valuable in your life. One thing to note is that the material world is a losing game from the start. Someone will always have a nicer, newer, and improved toy with better features, and the next guy will make more money than you. What then is valuable? What should we work on to secure true value? As mentioned, there are treasures that cannot be stolen, and that will surely last for as long as you live. Your value is in your gifts, skills, knowledge, abilities, and character. You are your own value and treasure, which you can either degrade or constantly upgrade.

Skills, gifts, talents, and abilities that are not used amount to nothing, but skills, gifts, talents that are used, refined every day, improved on, these will become your greatest joy, because only you know how to use them, no one can instruct you on how to use what is specifically and specially gifted to you.

Imagine that you are skilled or gifted in art and painting, you are able to charge R20 000 for doing one portrait because you know the effort, time, resources, and skills it took to do that portrait painting. But if you go work for someone or a company you will be told what you are worth and how much your work is worth. Put in mind that there are limits to how much an employer is willing to pay you for your skills and time. Therefore, seek to become a person of value. Value built by your uniqueness. By this I mean to seek to utilize the best that you can be at this very moment, only you can do better. Improve your talents and then make people pay you for them.

Things do not make you valuable, you make things valuable. Perfect examples for my statement are the Levis brand, Jordan clothes, Louis Viton, Ford (Henry Ford), Lamborghini (Ferruccio Lamborghini), Ferrari (Enzo Ferrari), Mercedes (Emil Jellinek's daughter Mercedes) and many more. You see these people are making clothes, cars, and other material things valuable by their names.

Today when you walk into a clothing store or car garage, we buy these names because they made them valuable by their name, their skills, vision, dream, and hard work. We buy people's value when we buy their brand of materials. How much are we paying to own one or more of the above names? That is why branding is so important. When things are branded, they sell at a much higher cost. What is your brand? What do you add to when you wake up in the morning?

I HAVE A QUESTION PLEASE

I was tempted not to touch the topic of success but something tells me that it is worth looking into since we looked at value. Looking at my opening quote from Einstein I also think that makes it a good topic to put our thoughts into. He says, "Try not to become a man of success but rather try to become a man of value." Try not to become a man of success? Wait what? I mean trying to become a man of success is my goal; it is all I ever know. It is in fact what I worked for my entire life, to become a man of success so that I may be respected and here you are telling me to try not to become a man of success. I then began to ask around what success meant or what success is to people around me.

What do you think are the first thoughts they had or what do you think are the first words that came out of their mouths? Try it yourself for the next five days at your employment environment, parties, meetings bedroom, or wherever you go, ask people what success looks like or how does a successful person looks like. Most answers you will get just like those I got will scream money. Making so much money per year or month and owning these and that, all the material gains which include expensive cars, huge houses, and luxurious clothes, climbing the corporate ladder and becoming the CEO of some big corporation, owning your own business and maybe having a family.

IT'S JUST A RUMOR

We heard in the past and the present people trying to explain what success is in their own way, mostly it was explained differently per individual. There is nothing wrong with that because success could be many things to different people. Let us further explore the topic of success. Success definition differs from individuals across the world. Take for example a student who wants to complete his four-year degree course, a writer who wants to write six books every year, a teacher who wants kids to get higher grades, a man who only wants to have a family, a person who stole expensive and valuable goods or you who want billions in your account.

Success means different things to each and every individual when you look at the above examples. Tesla says that a man is happy on the day he is born and the day that he finds out what he is born to do and the completion of that he was born to do. That is some good way to sum it up, but we can still simplify that. If you look at my examples in the opening you will notice that with a student, he wants to complete his four-year degree, the fruit or rewards depend on the completion. His success is realised only after completion of all the work he put forth. For a person who steals, something must be stolen; the rewards are dependent on the completion of the heist. The effort he puts in to complete the heist will determine his success. If he does not put in the work to finish his mission, he will not be successful.

The teacher wants higher grades for students, the student must complete for the reward to be realised. You see everything must be completed for it to earn the title of success and when it is complete it becomes a product of the work put in. You cannot be successful without putting in the work and more importantly completing the work. So, do you understand that success is not things or money? It is in the subtle things that cannot be explained in words or by just looking on the outside. It is deeper than that.

Only the people who have really tasted success will understand what I am communicating here. Your success depends entirely on you to manifest the best you can be. No one is going to show your abilities, skills, and capacity to win but yourself. Do not let me corner you into believing what success is by my definition, you have to define it for yourself, but when you do, please be careful not to attach materials or money into the definition.

A perfect example to question the common view of success is the story of Joseph in the book of Genesis. Moses tells us that Joseph was bought by Potiphar to be a slave in Egypt. When Joseph was bought, he was a slave in slave's clothes. Despite that Moses wrote to say that the "Lord was with Joseph, and he was a successful man." Think about that for a moment, he is a slave, but yet he has been called "SUCCESSFUL." This must make you think differently. What is success if a slave who has nothing is called "SUCCESSFUL"? For you and I if we are to be in that position, and we hear that we are called successful, we would burst into laughter or get very angry thinking that we are being ridiculously mocked.

Why then was Joseph called successful? It is simple, his greatness and success were trapped in him. The very path that he was on, despite being utterly hopeless, was his path to lead him to be the success that he already was. You are just the same. Your success is trapped inside of you. You are like a seed of a tree, flower, or any plant. For the tree is trapped inside the seed, and for the tree to become fully a tree that you and I can see, it must go underground. For some time, you cannot see it. It must let go of the state of being a seed then begin to manifest its true nature slowly. Your success is trapped in you. Just because people cannot tell that you are successful in all your ways, it does not mean you are not. For you to be visible you must exercise patience and hard work to complete what you must become. This throws away all the theories of referring to external material things as a success. These are just what I call gains. You gained or acquired the material things for enjoyment after you completed what you were tasked to do. You will notice that what you give and add to mankind is also an effort of success.

MONEY AND POSSESSIONS ARE OUT OF THE EQUATION

"The man who identifies himself with his possessions will feel that all is lost when these are lost; he who regards himself as the outcome and the tool of circumstances will weakly fluctuate with every change in his outward condition, and great will be his unrest and pain who seeks to stand upon the approbation of others." – James Allen

When you die you leave all your money and possessions to someone - a family member or charity to inherit. This is a good example. Everything you called success goes to someone else when you die. Would you say that the inheritor is successful when they inherit your materials, money, and titles? No. For them to be successful, they must manifest their greatness, skills, talents and abilities to build a good name for themselves.

Success, status and educational accolades and certificates cannot be inherited. David Oyedepo makes a joke in one of his sermons to say that perhaps your father was a heavyweight wrestling champion and willed his belt to you. It means you inherit his championship title. Now you are challenged to defend that title against a professional wrestler, what do you think will happen to you? So now you understand that success is deeply rooted in internal things than external material things.

Therefore, success must never be defined by money, having a nice car, big house, expensive clothes, and all the cool luxurious toys. Let's take a clear, honest fresh look at these concepts or the idea of success. What is the common understanding of success? Is it someone who ranks high in the company? Your job and title can be lost at any time on any given day. When you do your purpose-driven work, you do not have to worry about being fired, you do not retire from your work. But with your job, you retire and basically do nothing. With your work on the other hand, you do it until your death bed. I strongly believe that you will die a sweet death, knowing that you gave your best and all to the world.

DO NOT MISUSE SUCCESS

Success is good, accomplishments are good. The obstacle that we create and need to be aware of is using previous success to blind us from the possibility of future success. Many become so proud and excited about their achievements to a point that they cannot move on to their next accomplishments. It is important to not make that mistake. That is how success becomes misused; it becomes a tool to judge one's self against other people's successes.

This becomes a problem; it is a problem you create when not very careful. You find people under pressure because they want to catch up with a friend's success. People fall into financial struggles because they want to look successful. Seek that every good thing that you do have a long-lasting impact and have a sense of value-adding result to people. May your life, character efforts, and your very existence be not just writing upon the sand, here today and gone tomorrow but an engraving upon the rock that people look up to!

May you build your life on the material that is able to withstand hard times and fierce fires of anything that exist to oppose your very greatness that you were meant to be. May you be rooted and grounded in acts of love and support for one another so that we put away the blame of what is not going right but begin to sing praises of what is going right stimulated by our acts of taking responsibility. May your whole life be so value-driven and established that the history books remember your name.

Chapter 13 Change Is Growth And Development

*"As the seed is contained in the flower, and the flower in the
seed, so the relation of course and effect is intimate and
inseparable"— James Allen*

You were once one year older; today you are 23, 40, or 59 years
older. You were 120.5 cm tall, today you are 160 or 175.5 cm. This
is growth that whether you like it or not, will happen to you. You
cannot avoid growth or change in your life. No doubt you are going
to grow and develop in some way during the time given to you on
earth. It is unfortunate that most people grow older biologically but
never grow up and develop mentally and spiritually. Mental and
spiritual growth does not happen by chance or automatically. At
this early stage, we must deeply understand the difference between
development and growth. Growth will happen to you whether you
like it or not, it is natural to grow. Development on the other hand
is a result of choice; it means you choose to develop yourself.

Development is so much powerful because you choose it in areas you see fit. You control what goes in and out of your developmental system. With growth, you cannot just choose to be tall or choose not to grow, the process of growth will happen to you whether you like it or not.

Development is quite a challenge sometimes because it requires putting more effort, more hours, sacrifice, and a strong focus. I like using athletes as an example because I regard them up there in the ranks of disciplined and focused individuals. An athlete works out 6 to 8 hours, practice laps to develop physical strength and ability. You go to school to develop your mind; you read books and do research to develop your level of knowledge.

You choose development. While you are developing, growth of some kind takes place. Going back to development, you must be willing to work on your development. Feed both your spirit and mind with food suitable for such forces. It takes some serious intention and commitment to develop and grow. It is not a matter of want; it is a need for you to hunger for development. Decide now, today to develop tremendously, put plans in motion and exert some effort to develop, and continue on that road. Remember, we spoke about "discipline," this is where you will need to exercise your self-discipline.

The best thing to do for yourself is to learn this now. Learn this as quickly as you can and then choose the type of development that is suitable for you. The sooner you know that you are going to develop and grow, the better you become as you start choosing how you want to develop. There is certainly growth that is under your influence and the growth that will take its course by the law of nature. For example, your body will develop as you add age to your life. You were once an infant, you started to crawl, walk and today you are able to also run.

These changes did not happen overnight; it took some time. The plans you have for your future will take time. The development stage in any area of your life will take time. Be patient with the process and enjoy it. Human life is so amazing when you study it. Take yourself and live as a perfect subject of study. Be still and aware, you will then begin to know many important aspects of your life which will lead you to good developments.

We all pass the stages of birth, childhood, teenage phase to adulthood, and then old age. During this time, we experience, sickness, joy, sadness, anger, healing, and many more. All these experiences were necessary. They provided you with significant knowledge and forces that helped to shape the "You" that you see today. I am privileged to have had an opportunity to watch my daughters grow and develop. I believe that most of you have experienced such joy and learning experiences with your children. From 0 to 4 months my daughters did not move much, they cried, ate, and slept a lot; 4 to 5 months later they started to sit on their own and, held their own feeding bottles. As they fed, they grew stronger. Six to seven months later they started teething and began to stand on their feet, then they crawled, and now they are walking and trying to speak.

Soon they will be talking fully and will then start doing things by themselves, like bathing and requesting for food when feeling hungry. They will want to learn how to write, read, and so on. This is the process of growth that all of us have to go through. As they grow and develop, I also witness that they are starting to observe what is happening around their environment. Sometimes when I say and do something, they will attempt to do as I do. That is the part that is so natural to us to help us develop. We naturally have a force that kicks in to learn new things from our environments, experiences, and more.

I like the teachings of Myles Munroe. He used seeds as examples during his teachings. Let us look atone of his examples for perfect understanding and a clearer picture. Look at a seed, a seed of an avocado. It is a seed and within itself, it holds the potential to grow into a big avocado tree that will produce great avocados. You have the seed in your hand. The law of a seed says it needs soil, water, and sunlight. Therefore, you are going to need an environment to put that avocado seed in. The avocado is planted in soil, a good environment, not just any environment. The seed will not grow in a poor environment.

The avocado seed must then under the solid die of its seediness to become roots. That process takes time. You will not see what is happening, but you know a tree will come out. You do not leave your seed unattended; you water it and give it all the necessities it needs to grow from within. Fertilizers are what you will use for your seed to get nourishment. A month later you will see a little tip of your seed sprung from the ground, now you see that your tree is growing. You will continue to water it, give it sunlight and fertilizer, prune it, and remove weeds around it.

Your tree begins to grow slowly but it is guaranteed that there is a tree growing that one day will produce and give you avocados. This process of growth takes time, you cannot force the growth, laws of growth, nature must take place. The above process can be applied to your dreams, goals, and plans. You need a good environment to grow; you need fertilizers, such as your education, knowledge, food, love, and care and fun activities.

It takes time and discipline to fully become the best you, but rest assured you are getting there. During this process you will have to make choices, you are pruning and taking out weeds. You are having only good thoughts, keeping company with great minds, reading and taking care of your health, and so on. You stand in a more advantageous position because you have the power to choose your area of growth, and this is when development starts taking place. As to how far do you want to push your development that is entirely in your hands.

CHOOSE YOUR GROWING SEED WITH CAUTION

My question is if you take a seed of corn, plant it underground, follow all its laws and procedures for the seed to grow, what will eventually come out of that corn seed? A carrot? Or an apple or cabbage? Of course, none of the mentioned will come out of the corn seed except corn. It is impossible for the banana to come out as well. Corn will be produced by corn; it is that simple. That is why James Allen says nothing will come out of corn but corn. Nothing will come out of good, but good.

Nothing will come out of wealth, but wealth. Every seed planted brings forth its own multiplied. If I were you, I would start now to plant seeds of prosperity, seeds of hope, good, wealth, and other joyful rewards that life has to offer. What do you think will come out? The answer today will determine your chances of flourishing. This should remind you of Chapter 5, the universal laws.

You are a seed; your future and all your potentials are inside of you. If you take a corn seed and put it on your side bed table for over ten years, what will become of that seed? It will remain a seed because it was never used for its purpose. The purpose of a seed is to be planted, it needs soil and water. Choose to be idle with your life, and you will not become the great person you are meant to be. Begin working day and night to manifest what you are to become. If you do not, you will remain the same. You need knowledge; you need resources to guide you in your growth and development. That is why people like me exist, to help you grow and develop to the best you can be.

CHALLENGES ARE GOOD MOTIVATION FOR DEVELOPING AND CHANGING

In the midst of challenges is you will grow and develop more; you will build character and discipline. The process of building a character is a very slow process. That is why your ability to be patient will come in handy. Please try not to escape or avoid challenges, you need them. When you try to avoid, escape and play duck and dive with challenges, you are actually doing more harm to yourselves, you are delaying the process of growth and development, and you might end up with more struggles and pain.

Embracing the challenges, embracing the change, and taking full responsibility to allow you to develop much sooner and build a character that will last a lifetime. When this happens, you know that you are no longer a person seeking to be pitied you are now maturing into someone who takes control of their very own life. The things to remember about the process of growth and development.

For growth to take place, change must happen.

It takes time to grow and develop, just like a seed needs time to germinate.

Discipline and patience are required to be fully successful in developing.

Knowledge and understanding will always be the best ingredients in the process of change and development.

Invest in yourself to grow and develop.

Work on the things that manifest your best skills, abilities, and character.

Chapter 14 The Ark: Preparation

"Go to the ant, you sluggard! Consider her ways and be wise... Provides her supplies in the summer and gathers her food in the harvest. How long will you slumber, O sluggard when will you rise from your sleep?"— Proverbs

We touched the preparation aspects in the previous chapters. We will go even deeper into preparation in this chapter. There is no building that can stand firm without a solid foundation and no single tree that can stand without roots. There is no great performance without practice and no success without planning and action. There is no physical strength and fitness without exercising. Everything you desire to accomplish has preparation stages. I find the story of Theodore Roosevelt a very good example packed with life lessons. He flourished in times of crisis and challenges.

It is being said that despite being privileged, he suffered many misfortunes when growing up. He had Asthma. His Asthma attacks were so severe that he nearly died. He worked out at the gym his father built for him, strengthening his body to beat asthma that left him weak in bed for more than weeks. By the time he was a young adult, his asthma was eradicated. What did he do? He prepared his body for the future. His story does not end there. Roosevelt lost his wife, his mother, and nearly lost his life in a fatal assassination attempt. He suffered many election defeats, he had political enemies and during his time of office the nation was faced with a great depression and wars, he survived because he prepared at an early age, his preparation was not only physical, he prepared his mind and emotions.

Another great preparation example is that of Noah. Noah did not know the exact date of the flood, but he prepared for it. Days and days, he worked to build the ark. People mocked him. No one had ever seen rain in the time of Noah. To them, it was a joke, but Noah knew that the storm was going to come at its appointed time. When the storm came Noah was prepared. He was safe because he paid heed to the advice and instructions from God. He did not react to change, he responded to change because of the early obedience to prepare for the storm. They say Noah was faithful to God.

When people gave in to debauchery, Noah stood up with faithfulness. Look what righteousness and faithfulness earned Noah. Is your faith fully committed to your goals? Are you obedient to take advice for your life? Do you invest time in building reservoirs that can save your life, save money, invest in education and knowledge, build good relationships? Are you ready for change and crisis?

Do you develop skills that can pay for your future needs? If you are not doing any of the above, do not be afraid, but begin working on it now. It is very likely that in your case it won't be the same storm of Noah's time. You might not face the same challenges as Roosevelt but whatever comes your way, you must be ready. You do not know when the storm of the financial crisis, recession, layoffs, ill health, loss of a spouse, or loved one, will hit you; you do not know what will happen five years from now to the company you signed a contract with.

As I mentioned, change will happen and problems will exist. When the problem comes, take up the challenge and change to meet that problem and benefit from the change, don't be afraid. I remember in my early school years when I had to prepare for a test or examination. It was not exciting to study or prepare, because I was young and naive. Until I grew up and learned that life's reality is not as sweet as I imagined, I began to value hard work. I started to prepare myself for the future. Spiritual, emotional, physical, and mental preparations became part of my life.

Every day there I was, reading, meditating, and taking action. The word from the book of life is the number one tool to start with as you work your way around physical preparation. When you delight in the word, study it day by day, you automatically equip yourself with the strength that you may never think possible. You also prepare yourself for future trials.

Kenneth Copeland calls these preparation acts "making a deposit", making a deposit so that when the time of need arises your heart and mind will be so deeply established and rooted in strength that your first response will not be of fear, but of faith and trust knowing that everything will work out for good because you have stored good treasures that will see you through in hard times. When the hour of trial arrives, you will feel a better person because you know that your life is established on something more powerful than any change or problem. You will have peace and enough strength to work everything out.

ALWAYS INITIATE PREPARATION, LET IT BE A HABIT

Preparation requires practice and voluntary acts. Here is why it is important for you to engage voluntarily in preparation. Number one is that when you prepare voluntarily you learn well and enjoy the learning. When you learn under pressure you only learn fast and only for that momentary conditions which at a later stage your learning will not be enough. For example, if you are forced to save your life or the life of a loved one you will improvise and use all your abilities to save a life without learning much because everything was done in a rush under an intense condition.

Now when you take your time to learn, for example. First Aid and your Cardiopulmonary resuscitation (CPR), when the need arises to use such skills you will do it with ease because you learned by choice not under some intense pressure. Even better you are able to transfer the skills to others to save lives as well.

BENEFITS OF PREPARATION

When you prepare, you will always be at peace.

You can never fail the test when prepared.

You are never afraid but full of confidence and control. It has been said that life is the best teacher, but I stand to disagree. Life gives you trials before it equips you with knowledge. In reality, things are different; you do not get an announcement to warn you in advance about the next challenge or crisis. You do not get a warning of an accident or robbery, or when your car will breakdown, but you must be prepared.

PREPARATION THEME

I was a young man, during my young years I stumbled and fell. I fell far too many times to count, the bruises and injuries healed and with every fall I became wiser and stronger. Oh, I wish elders would replace worry with teaching, how I wish someone told me that it will never be easy. For life, lessons are not so tender as the love of a parent. The lessons were not pleasant, so I sought out to voluntary learning This gave me little comfort; little did I know that there is no comfort for a soldier. I decided that before any fall could happen, I must always be ready. There I was like a soldier going to battle, I laboured day and night, immersed myself in the study of life.

*Little did I know that my labour will transform a young man
into a great man. With patience and precision, I paid with
heart and soul Today I am not a young man nor am I full of
age but I am strong and wise. The trials of life still come and
go, I give no regard to them because my victory is assured.
Oh, I will teach my children, for my love is so tender and the
lessons will be enjoyable. They will not wish for anything
because I will be there to tell them that it is easy. I am better,
I know better and I do better.*

*I did not like living like a soldier preparing for a war that I
will never understand but in the end, there is not much to be
understood. With every battle won, war became a friend. I
still fight the good fight for war will not end, I know that
someday I will have to put my guns down, when that day
comes, I want you to pick up the guns and fight on because
that is the way of life. There you will be like a soldier going to
battle, you will labour day and night, immersing yourself in
the study of life. If only you knew that your labour will
transform a young man into a great man. you will pay the
price with heart and soul*

Chapter 15 Embrace Chance

Chances are to be created, use optimistic lenses and you will find yourself exuberating in everlasting victory.

Chance is your heartbeat, the blink of an eye, the speed of light, chance is in every breath you take, it is always there, waiting, bring it to be and you will be exalted; chance is a friend of the opportunist who is always seeking. Perhaps your next step will lead you to the right door for that very step is chance. No morning and night can come without chance, like a song it rhymes, waiting for those who will listen, can you hear that, can you hear it? It is calling out for those who love victory. You are able to create your own chances.

I learned this truth from watching a very inspiring film "Lord of War", Nicholas Cage starred in the film. At a particular time during his life in the film, he had to create an important chance to get him closer to his goal. His goal was a woman, reality told him that there was no way he could get anywhere close to her considering that they were worlds apart one was a pure warlord and the other was a young attractive model living the dream.

Nicholas did not listen to the whispers of reality but went on to defy reality by taking matters into his own hands. He understood the unstoppable power behind creating chances. I think that is why he said "You can't force someone to fall in love with you but, you can definitely improve your odds." He worked out a plan, went all out to create events that eventually led him close to his goal. What do you think happened? He got what he wanted; he got the girl. Of course, it was all in a film but the principles apply in real life. I do not think of a better way to get to your goals than creating chances that favour your plans. Remember, you cannot force things to go your way but you can improve your odds.

THE WAIT IS OVER
Chance is the next moment. Every moment is the first, another opportunity to turn your life around. The moment you have now is the best powerful moment you will ever have or stand-in, in your life. There will never be a moment like the one you have now. You have the power to choose, to make a choice to reach your dreams.

Chance is created not given. It's well-known today that success, accomplishments, or getting ahead do not happen by luck or by spinning a coin. If that is your thinking then I hate to be the bearer of sad news, that won't get you anywhere in life. You have to plan and work out every detail to achieve your goal. Only you can make it happen, you start by creating chances that favour your plans.

It is important to notice that you cannot separate chance from change and change from chance, the two work together. For change to take place opportunity or a chance must be presented and then you can succeed. Those that are waiting for friends, family, or lightning to strike for them to make changes, they are in for a very long wait. Work out your own salvation, Adam Khoo mentioned that at the age of 15, he already had a detailed plan for his future written out. When you are specific about your plans you will begin to attract resources to aid you to achieve those plans. It is in smaller steps, plans, and day to day activities that you achieve your ultimate goals. Once I learned this truth, I never wasted a single day of my life. I started creating chances for myself. I got fascinated by how easy life became when I created my own opportunities, initiated actions, and accomplished small tasks I set for myself.

Day by day I got attracted to the idea of succeeding; I turned every stone and every rock to learn how to lead a successful life. Through research and information, I consumed, I came across some life-changing knowledge. I came to learn of the extraordinary lives of people all over the world who revolutionized the world. The likes of Elon Musk, Mark Zuckerberg, Warren Buffet, Bill Gates, Alexandra the Great, Franklin Roosevelt, and many more. It is obvious that I am mentioning billionaires, millionaires, and great historical leaders. There is a good reason why.

If you study a billionaire's biography you will never stop and most importantly you will understand that their success did not happen by luck but through dedicated hard work, a lot of risk-taking, and trying over and over again. Things like reading books, taking risks, and setting new goals to stretch their limits are very common among these great men. But the knowledge that stole my heart during this quest is that almost all of them said to create your own future by taking risks and creating chances and use your mind. The mind is one tool that gets you started with everything. A start to greater things if not for everything.

FROM MIND TO CHANCES

The subject of learning about the human mind captivated me so much that I dedicated my days to that specific study and nothing more. Books, TV shows, podcasts, almost everything I worked on were to either be able to take control of the activities of the brain or to learn about it. Remember what I said about beliefs, is that they guide your life. In the back of this mind that I am researching, I knew that if I became the master of my mind then it would be easier for me to create chances that favoured my goals.

I believe that if I was able to change and control my mind. I knew that I had to work; I knew that nothing will come as easy as I wanted it to. So, I worked. The good thing is that I had direction, I knew what to do and I set out to do it. My attitude is what kept me going. Every time I remembered how far I'd come; I would push myself even more I pushed. I put my mind to work extra, I knew that this alone was another way for me to get closer to my goal.

Tim Grover is Michael Jordan's Coach. He says that "the body has limitations, the mind does not have limitations, we focus so much on what goes from the neck down that we forget that it all starts with the mind. Everything starts with the mind, if you are not mentally ready you are never physically prepared. That is where the preparations start, in the mind." This is so true; I just love the fact that my mind can take me anywhere, this means I can create every chance I can think of. That is why Paul encourages us to renew our minds so that we may be transformed to be new creatures.

Today I am a new creature, but this could have not happened if I did not create chances for myself. This could have not happened if I did not make a choice to use my mind to create opportunities. Everything that is going right in my life is the fruits of my mind's work supported by the chances that I create. Coming to you dear reader, I believe without a doubt that you also possess this powerful force to create what matters to you. I want you to know wherever you are, that you can do it and I support you a hundred percent. If you have a goal that you want to reach but do not know where to start, I encourage you to contact me so that we can help each other to get you closer to your goal. This will be fun for you. I can't wait to hear from you dear reader.

Chapter 16 Get Serious, Life Is No Joke

"Whoever pursues righteousness and love finds life, prosperity, and honor." — Proverbs

I t is man's important task to find out what to do with his life. I believe in second chances; even better I believe that a person can get thousands of chances. One thing I know for sure is that in all the chances we get whether second or tenth chance, life does not give you a rehearsal session, you get only this one treat and that is the end of it. Life is serious, there is no time to swim with the tide, you will swim with the tide to the north and later find out that you were called to go south. By the time you row back to the south, it is already too late. Do not be fooled by comfort of the words like, "it is never too late," because sometimes it is too late. Let me give you something to think about.

You grow old biologically, some of the things that you are able to do very well now at your young age, some you will no longer have the abilities to do very well later when you are full of age because of simple biological factors. You may get better physically as you grow sometimes yes, but your physical status may deteriorate at some point in time. So please do what is important now while you are still fit, young and strong. That is why it is important to get down to the core of life and start digging and creating

Gold is never found in the surfaces; you have to dig deeper to find fine gold, diamonds, and rubies; you have to swim deep into the heart of the oceans to find treasures. When you do find your gold, diamonds, and treasures, I tell you that there will never be a day wasted in your life; you will want to do more. Your purpose, goals, and dreams are your fine gold and diamonds. What they told you when growing up that it is OK to not know what you want or what to do with your life is no longer a good song to sing. It is time to change the tune and know what you want. Frustrations come easier when your life has no sense of purpose, value, or when you have no goals to work on. This is not how you should live your life; it is one of man's important tasks to find out what he wants and what to do when he finds it. Normally a person who goes with the flow is frustrated and restless.

DEFINITELY THERE IS MORE TO LIFE THAN GOING WITH THE FLOW

Imagine living for more than 25 years of your life going with the flow, with no goal, vision, or meaningful work. There is got to be more to life than swimming with dead fish. I, therefore, encourage you to think and re-evaluate your life because if you do not, you will be distracted and be carried away by everybody's business. The world is so busy, the only way for you to have peace is to identify your why (the reason for living) and start working on it till you get the results you want.

The danger of not having clear goals and no sense of vision is that you will start experimenting with your life and some experiments are irreversible. Having a clear goal and plan and purpose, you shield yourself from lots of misfortunes. When you know where you are going, automatically you know where not to go, who not to speak to, and all other activities that you should not do. Anything that does not add to your goal and plans you will not consider because the minute you entertain such, you will be side-tracked. I hope you take this seriously and start working on your life now.

FOLLOW THE LIGHT IN YOUR HEART

One day you will look at yourself and be thankful for identifying your plans while it is still early. If you are already old, do not despair, it's not late to do certain things. For those that you can still do, go on to make an impact with your life, and give your best. It is your job from this day on to find out why and what. I believe it is easy because there is one thing that you have in your heart that just lights up your face when you think about it, follow that light.

Get yourself focused, start working on the things that will give you peace, and add value to the rest of your remaining days. Be clear, and specific of your paths. What you are searching for will be found within. Find your connection to the higher power, and your inner person and then take advantage. The universe is always willing to help those who seek.

For you to start working on something worthwhile, you must prepare. You must ready yourselves for the challenges to come. It will put you at ease to understand where you are and where you want to go. Right now, all you have is time and this life. Both life and time are so precious that when wasted, one grieves. Use your time and this one life that you have very well.

That is why I say life is serious, sure we can have fun and joke around but when all is said and done your life needs to matter or count for something. The reality behind the connection of our dreams, goals, plans, love, friendships, family, laughter, fun activities, challenges, death, money and what we do not know but yet to know is what keeps us together, it is what gives our life sense and meaning; the reason to waking up, to go do something.

While it is necessary to take it easy sometimes, it is even more necessary to work hard. I laugh quietly every time when I hear someone saying: "I am taking things easy; I'm going with the flow." Remember what I said earlier in this chapter that there is simply no time to go with the flow, only dead fish go with the stream.

My question is how can you take it easy when you have no sense of direction? I advise you to be aggressive and strongly pursue the matters of your life before it gets late. Look, I understand that you cannot have everything figured out, but you must have at least a few things figured out. There are lots of uncertainties especially when you do not know which direction to take. It is scary but that is where most life happens.

Taking a chance with the unknown, choose one way and giving your all, regardless of what comes. Right there you will find the joy of living. The thrill and the joy of life mostly come from taking a challenge without knowing what the journey will be like. Development and growth coupled with learning and strength will be manifested in you when you take this approach. Think of any point in your life when you had to make a very important decision in your life. Did you know what hand the future will deal to you? Did you know what the journey would be like? Absolutely no, you did not know all of that, but you made a decision. It ended up paying off. If it did not pay off, try again or learn whether it is worth it or not.

For you to not get lost in the practice of going with the flow you must put proper preparations in order. Take for example someone who wants to pick a course of study at university or someone who wants to start a business or someone who wants to take a traveling trip. All of these people have something in common, a goal in mind. They must all prepare step by step to see that their goals are achieved. For someone who wants to go to university, he must make sure that he meets the requirements of the course, and must have a tuition fee. The person who wants to take a traveling trip must have a destination, means of transport and the reason to travel.

You must commit to at least one destination in your life. Note that your commitment to that destination is not a permanent matter. Goals and dreams change, one day you wake up with thoughts of starting afresh, and you go on to do it. The point I am trying to communicate is that you must have something going on in your life. If you do not commit to something, you will wake up one day regretting it. The time is now for you to make things right for yourself. I mean they say "it's OK to not have a plan" but I tell you now that, that is not good advice. Have a plan; if you do not have one, start now to work it out. I am not saying you should have all the answers for your life, but you should at least have a plan to try and find answers. There is no time to waste.

We are given time in this world, but none of us knows when it's going to shut us out. Have a meeting with yourself, if you do not have anything or anyone to push you to become your best. Be that someone or something to yourself. Why do you think we work so hard to get the best life care, nourish our bodies, we try by all means to stay out of dangerous environments, avoid threatening circumstances, and people that make us feel unhappy? It's because we care, we care for ourselves, we care for our lives and above all, we love life despite all the challenges. Take it seriously today, work on the things that matter most to you, and work on the things that will develop your life, empower yourself and guard your steps.

Work first for what is right and then for what is good, for that will not only benefit you but also the surrounding people. Some say that "you have all the time" and people go-ahead to think that they do have time and then later when they fail to reach their goals they come back and say "but I do not have time" or "I had little time." You confuse yourself in the process. Instead of assuming, get down to the core of your life and work. Delight yourself in the joy of discovering the value of your life; add to the world your best works.

Chapter 17 Embrace The Man: Hidden Treasures

I It is not the goals, the plans, and the problems that matter, at the end of the day it is the man that matters because, without man, problems, goals, dreams, and plans do not exist. When you set out your course of life, make it a priority to take care of the man, get to know the man, feast with the man, laugh with the man, get angry at the man, forgive the man, and love the man.

Understand the man. You will then see that life is about the man and what he can add to this life. That leads to questions, what can a man do? What is the purpose of the man? What makes a man? Answer these questions.

I do not know you but I can promise that if you answer those questions you will find joy in your life. All your problems and life struggles will be over because you have known the man.

You are the best thing to happen to this world, own it, and make something of that. When one realises that it is close to impossible for him to succeed in all his endeavours to change the world before knowing himself, he then, with patience and diligence starts to seek knowledge and wisdom that leads to self-discovery. He begins to look inside, day by day blossoming from within, with every step he takes to know himself. This then allows him to become the victor in life because he sees now that for the world to change, it begins with him.

It is the deeper things that you cannot see when you look in the mirror that make you a greater being. When you stop to complain about the trials of life and begin to embrace each trial as another step to self-discovery and self-development, the universe starts assisting you. Very important to understand is that you must get to the level of self-awareness before you can start moving mountains. Know your own strengths and flaws then work hard to perfect your strengths. This is one key for you to get to the next level of life. Begin everything by being grateful, when you begin to be grateful and trust that life will only bring good to you, you open up every channel of blessings to come your way. When things go out of plans, you can choose not to fret because you know for sure that the power is right within you.

Each day should begin with a purpose and building strength with every victory or defeat. Right now, where you are at this very moment, you have within you great treasures that can change the world. Treasures that can change the course of life as we know it, treasures that can change everything we ever believed in, treasures that can open a whole new chapter and destiny for everyone around you. The treasures that are locked inside of you can turn your loss into gain, poverty to prosperity, despair into hope, sickness into health, sorrow into joy, and emptiness to a filled life of purpose.

It is your responsibility to search, keep looking, and opening new doors until you find your treasures. In fact, your treasures need not be found but manifested because they are already in you. You just have to be bold enough to take the route of wisdom and self-awareness to manifest your potentials to the fullest. Only you have the keys and only you will know which doors the keys can open. Everything you ever wanted and desired is right there within your reach to claim because it is your prerogative to do so. The next best thing to do when you find your treasure is not to keep such amazing treasures to yourselves but share them with those who understand and are ready to receive. You should not keep the light and your best gifts to yourselves.

DO NOT SHINE ALONE; A MILLION MORE NEED YOUR SPARK OF HOPE

The act of giving back is the best thing you can do when you have found the ecstasies of life. You should give back so that others can also find and share their joy. Remember that for you to shine and get a breakthrough more is expected from you; you have a responsibility to teach others because there are many who need the same light. Teach the next person and be there for someone.

You will be surprised by how much change you can bring about for people who are willing to receive knowledge and guidance. Plant hope in the hearts of your neighbours and friends instead of quarrelling. The acts of inspiring, giving hope, empowering those who want to be empowered, will make a better society if not a better world. Spread the inspiration and knowledge into the hearts of all who want to receive. Share opportunities with them for in so doing you will then change the world as we know it. It starts with the man; it starts with the man digging within and becoming self-aware by starting to love the truth, knowledge, and loving life itself.

When you love life, you cherish every single aspect of it be it a natural thing or man-made thing. Everything becomes precious to you when you begin to step into the higher realm of self-awareness. You have, within you the power to really change the world.

MEETING WITH THE ONLY IMPORTANT PERSON IN THE WORLD

Sitting in a meeting, the chairperson would open the meeting by welcoming everyone present, giving apologies for those who did not make it. The agenda for the meeting was circulated a week before. Everyone at the meeting knows what the meeting is about and what we hope to achieve. Those who are responsible for reporting prepared their presentations and reports. The chairperson would announce the purpose of the meeting, putting emphasis on the progress reports on this and that for small talk sometimes but at the very same time trying to remind everyone how important the meeting is.

Chairperson would then begin to explain the agenda points and how we would go about the agenda. If there was a previous meeting, the matters of the previous meeting would be reviewed and attended to. Then on the agenda, we tackle the points as they are listed.

With every point, we would discuss, give feedback, and set the next goals with targets and time frames regarding points that need such attention. When this is done, we would then set up the date for the next meeting to report. Your life at some level should be conducted much the same. Make it a must for you to hold frequent meetings to report to yourself on how you are managing and leading your life. A report must be ready on time; you must be able to know the progress in your life. This is not only about progress but also to identify challenges that prevent you from rising to new heights.

This will include setting up meeting dates, perhaps monthly or weekly. This act shows that you care more than enough for your life. You will be amazed by how much you will discover about yourself, in fact, you will surprise yourself in every meeting. You perhaps live with yourself but do not know how you look, and I am not talking about the shape of your head or that little scar on your cheek. I am talking about the real you. The real you that makes people love you regardless of any physical flaws. If you do not know how that person looks, you will one day wake up not recognizing yourself because you never made time to meet with the most important person in your world. Set a date, set up your own agenda, and do not meet with yourself without setting points of discussion because if you do not, you will be tackling a lot of things at once.

The reporting time will also present to you with opportunities to reflect on the distance that you have travelled. The reflection will always be filled with questions, confrontations, corrections, and remedies. I hope by now you are saying, "Rorisang, I get it now, I should arrange a meeting with myself, prepare my agenda points for discussion, and ready myself to report, just like the example in the opening of this section. I get that the meeting with me is important and probably the most important meeting I will ever have in my life."

If you understand how important it is to reflect with yourself, then you are on the right track. This meeting will require you to have a non-judgemental attitude and try as much as possible not to beat yourself up when you do not get the answers right away. Be clear and stay focused. Using a mind map is a good approach if you want to get the best insight if agendas are not your thing. I prefer the mind map approach rather than a list of item points. In that way the mind map allows me to put myself in the center of my life and attach the center with things like goals, challenges, resources, people who can help, and so on. See my example in the picture below. Create a mind map for yourself also touching the most important aspects of your life. This is a technique that will give you peace of mind and more understanding of your life. If you are new to a mind map idea do not worry yourself, it is quite an easy thing to do. Just use Google, search for words, "mind map" and see what comes out. You will see something like the picture below. You just need to adjust and start doing it the way you see fit.

Mind   **Map:**
Meeting

illustration

Your mind map does not have to be perfect or well-drawn; it just has to make sense to you to make sure that you understand what is happening in your life. Things will always change; your mind map will somehow guide you. This can be used for just about anything from goal setting to resolving complex matters. I just prefer using mind maps for progress purposes specifically to see what is happening with my life. Your case could be different. You are not limited; use the mind map as you please so long as you produce results. Another example is to use the mind map for working on a specific goal. Looking at the above picture you can replace the "YOU" with "GOAL." Just as you are in the middle, this time it is your goal that is in the middle. You can list what you need to act on or you can list what you have done so far regarding the goal. What are the challenges, remedial actions, how far do you still need to? What have you achieved for yourself so far and what are you doing about the challenges presented? Some plans you might want to let go of. You might have good reasons to let them go or you might not have. It is OK, goals and plans change from time to time. That you should not worry about, you also should not worry about how messy your mind map looks. The important thing is that you capture all the points needed to help you get a step closer to achieving your goals.

MEETING THE PERSON IN THE MIRROR, THE ONLY ONE WHO CARES

Do not go looking for someone to care for you, your dreams, and goals. If I offer to provide you with free transportation, accommodation, and money to travel around the world to go look for that one person who cares about you more than anyone else, you will probably pack your bags and go, you will first enjoy the travel but in the end, you will not find that person anywhere but in the mirror. You can even take a second trip around the world if you think you missed something from the first trip. The answer will always come back to you.

That person in the mirror that you just give one look and forget how he/she looks like when you leave the mirror, is surely the only person who cares for you and is the only one who can help you. Go to your mirror and look beyond the skin, the eyes, and your square jaws, see what is really inside you. Ask yourself questions that will reveal your true nature, strengths, skills, abilities, and more. Surprise yourself by discovering you every day.

Discuss with yourself your needs and work out a plan to help yourself Look into the mirror, have a very good honest, challenging conversation that you can ever have in your life, it might probably be the first and most important honest reflection you will ever have. You owe it to yourself. Talk about yourself; ask the person you are looking at questions. When you feel like you need help, turn to the higher power for clarity and truth about yourself. It is your life, care enough to make a change and grow beyond measures.

Remember that you are doing it for you. No individual will help you get the answers you need. The idea of a meeting with yourself is solely to help you flourish and to help you achieve everything your heart desires. Very often the things that you do not see in your life when you look in the mirror are the very things that will help you get answers. Some amount of truth is required from you; in fact, the whole truth is required from you to pass the mirror test. Be as truthful and as honest as possible. This is one of the keys that will create a chance for you to succeed in everything you could ever want.

Write discoveries you find about yourself on paper. I do not care where you write them, but make sure they are written somewhere, write down, and review. When you are done, go and apply and put your strengths to work. Why is it important to embrace the man? "Don't freak yourself out by what other people have. They don't have what you've got." – Simon Sinek. The dictionary defines "embrace" as the act of showing affection and acceptance. Showing affection and acceptance takes a lot. In the process of showing affection and accepting, you are simply saying you love yourself and this is true in the case of others whom you extend your affection and acceptance to.

When you embrace the man (which is you of course), you begin to tap into new thinking that is more creative and you also tap into new understandings. Allow me to explain a little better for you to understand. Well since embracing the man requires you to accept and love yourself for who you are, it also means that you must let go of certain habits, thoughts, and actions that previously hindered your way to fully see yourself clearly.

The very act of letting go means liberty. It is close to impossible to be liberated without having knowledge and understanding. In other words, I am saying it will become a challenge if you try to let go of what you do not understand. The experience of freedom gives peace which allows your creative juices to work at their peak. This is good, it is good for you as an individual; for creativity plays a much greater role for your very survival and to reach new heights.

You will learn more about creativity and creating in the chapters to follow especially the chapter, "keys to flourish." It is easy to think that you are totally free. You may be thinking right now that you are, but are you? You might ask 'why do I have to be liberated when I am already free?' It is a good question and also it is very good to think that you are free. Let us ponder on the following question to see how true your claim to being free is. Do you feel jealous   at   times? Do you feel that you have the need to become better, wish that you could start afresh, perhaps let go of some past heavy memories? Of course, you must feel some of the above and because you do, you might have a need to be liberated from such feelings or thoughts. A man is always his own enemy that is why Paul said, that "we do not fight against the physical but against powers and principalities."

These powers and principalities are your memories, thoughts, guilt, depression, envy, jealousy, hurts, and other members of the same household. You are human and because of that, it is very likely that memories (good or disturbing) sometimes drive you insane. It is the work of the brain to store up some memories. Some memories have great influences in your life. The way you were brought up, the knowledge you have, the social, cultural, and religious environments you were exposed to, all have an impact on you and you have to let go and be free from what is holding you back.

A friend of mine said that "Truth has no path, it must be discovered from moment to moment; and you can discover it only when the mind is free, unburdened with the continuity of experiences." There is truth in that; you can only live up to your best when you have nothing holding you back.

When you embrace the man, all the past, ill burdens, and selfish desires fall away. Let us look at one example from this bold statement I am making. Think about envy for a moment. Envy is very common in our lives. Imagine a very good day, there you are tending to your garden, enjoying the pleasant smell of the flowers, and the sunlight. Your heart enjoys the melody coming from the birds, and the peace you have when you see different colours in your garden. The beauty of it all. Suddenly you notice that a neighbour is doing upgrades in their house. You are wondering how they are adding another story to the house. Another neighbour pulls out an expensive sports car from their garage. Like many, it is possible that you may also feel that you need to upgrade and perhaps own one of those nice sports cars or something. The minute you have such thoughts you lose the enjoyment and peace you had for your beautiful garden. The feelings of wanting to have what your neighbours have are taking over, that is envy right there. It can happen to anyone truly.

Sometimes it happens when you are in the streets. There you are driving to a grocery store. A shiny new Mercedes passes by; you begin to have desires to own the same. You forget you own a car that is taking you from place to place. Such feelings captivate you, prevent you to appreciate what you have; therefore, you also cannot think and see clearly. Going all out to get that new iPhone that a friend makes you desire one also. The constant struggle of comparison with others is on, the constant battle to get better than the next person is on and also, the need to have more in the hope of becoming happier or the need to keep up with the trending world.

The trap of envy and comparison leaves you with dissatisfaction. When you are dissatisfied you become less creative and less effective. The person inside you is left desolate. These traps and struggles rise when you do not accept yourself for who you are when you do not know yourself very well. When you have accepted yourself, you walk with confidence; you have trust in your abilities. You know what you can do and you are trusting in your own unique self. This allows you to not go with the masses but follow the very heart of your individuality. When you are at that peak of embracing your uniqueness, struggling with envy or desires is no longer a thing in your life. You become liberated; you no longer suffer any pressure.

Have you noticed that certain unsettling issues arise because you do not fully understand the person you are? The pressure of wanting approval from others locks you in day by day. You like the things that others like because you want to fit in, and I understand that very often we want to belong and be part of something. But this is a disaster friend. By doing what others do, you give away your freedom and power. Perhaps like me, you also grew up around uncles, friends, and a society where many are crazy about the same things. For example, in a group of friends, you find that they all love a BMW or a Mercedes. You convince each other that these are the best cars (maybe they are) and when you drive them, prestige follows you. The problem arises when one friend out of the group buys that car. Instead of being happy for a friend, and shower them with congratulations, a feeling of jealousy and envy comes in. You either become jealous or competitive.

The pressure and the envy would not be there if one embraces their uniqueness. You would perhaps love a Camaro instead of the Mercedes, and then you would just congratulate your friend and continue living without struggling with envy and pressure. This happens also in work environments because you have the same qualification, skills and probably went to the same school, you end up working in the same job competing for the same position

All these are real-life situations that happen when we neglect to embrace our uniqueness. It is more like a prison, which results in missing opportunities and recognizing the beauty of the great person you are. On a more personal level, with relationships, you have friends turning against each other and committing horrible acts towards one another because of the same taste and love in women or men. When one starts dating a certain person, the other wants to experience the same joy and for that reason, unnecessary strife between friends begins. All these happen because no one takes time to embrace the man.

When you truly understand that you are different and allow yourself to be guided by those unique qualities, you would not be pressured by competition. You won't be comparing yourself with anything or anyone. You will be sufficient for yourself. This is the society that we live in; we are conditioned to think that we are the same and it's OK to want to have what the next person has.

The benefits of embracing yourself in a pressured society will help you to cope. There won't be a need for you to go get yourself in credit because you have no pressure to buy that big mansion and own all-new luxuries. Peaceful living comes when one starts to work on himself. Like I said have a, meeting with yourself to understand why you are who you are. Understand your unique shape and design as a person and then use your unique design and shape to produce something that is truly you. You can get rid of the envy, comparison, pressure, and other ill behaviors that drive you insane. You will save yourself from doing dumb acts thinking that you will please or impress people. The truth is that you cannot win all hearts so if I were you, I would stop right now. This is one cure for escaping the people-pleasing weakness. When you embrace the man you no longer have a need for approval; that kind of fear and manipulation is no longer a worrying factor.

There are a lot of advantages when you embrace yourself, in fact, I choose to see only advantages, not downsides. Take time to get to know yourself and overcome the forced beliefs imposed by society, religion, social lifestyle, and the education system. Finding a way out won't be realised when you do what they say, what they do, or wanting what they want. Becoming them or like them won't help you, nor is using them as your measuring sticks; actually, the latter is worse.

APPRECIATING THE DIFFERENCES IN OTHERS

First things first, you will accomplish more than what you can ever imagine when you embrace the difference in others. Your differences complement each other to make progress. Where you are lacking the other is able to help you, "two are better than one," King Solomon said. Getting mingled with different thinkers is good for you. Learning to appreciate people different from us makes the world so much better. Appreciate differences in others but challenge common thinking for the purpose of understanding and seeking improvement. The answers to a better life lie within you. Free yourself from prejudices, pressures, and struggles. Putting it all together, you will understand that the freedom that I speak of is tied around many things that you do every day through thoughts and actions influenced by many things. Does this answer the question of why is it important to embrace the man? I believe it does. Surely right now I gave you something to think about. Reflect on the times when you felt the pain of envy, comparison, jealousy, and more. You will begin to realise that all that you need is to better understand who you are, more than anything.

When I speak of understanding who you are I do not speak of small things like what you like or do not like or what you may feel comfortable with. I speak of deep things that will reveal your strengths, abilities, and the resilient person that you are and most importantly the uniquely designed and perfect you. If you love popularity, and the praises of men mean more to you than adding value to society then you may have to carefully look deeper within yourself and change for the better. It is my belief that as human beings we cannot achieve and live up to our full potential if we are not ready to challenge the popular and common beliefs. The best part is that when we do challenge ourselves to move past limitations, we are able to manifest great acts and results that revolutionize the course of life as we know it.

Chapter 18 Official Guide And Driver: Vision

The world is built by visionaries; without them, we would not have all the beautiful things we enjoy today. Nelson Mandela, Martin Luther King Jr, Mother Teresa, Buddha, John F Kennedy, and many more held a vision, a dream to make the world a better place. Yes, their visions and dreams might have been different but the end results were almost the same; that is for all human race to stand on the common ground of love, peace, and prosperity. Today some of their visions have materialized and are cherished; we are living in a better world because of them. There were others such as Wright brothers who had a dream of having a flying machine. One hundred and fourteen years later, the airplane was invented. We have Elon Musk and Steve Jobs who are changing the world of technology. There are architects, artists, engineers who all have visions and dreams to make everything beautiful. Their visions began with a thought, and then materialized into the visible world you see today.

YOU ARE A VISIONARY

You are a visionary with all the superpowers to change anything you like; you do not have to have pressure to change the world but you can change and work on your ideas and dreams. Perhaps you want to work on your vocations, start a business, design and develop, build technology that can make things better, it could be anything. Whatever it is, you can do it. Embrace your visions, the fire that sparks in your heart, workday, and night to see your visions come to reality. Your visions are a very good sign that one day you will become a successful person if you work to manifest that vision.

SUPERPOWERS TO SEE BEYOND TOMORROW

Perhaps you have, at some point or another wondered why some people make it in life and why others do not get anywhere close to getting what they want. You may ask why there is so much progress in the lives of others around you but not in your life despite putting plans and actions in motion. Hard work is always the answer no doubt, but hard work won't be much enjoyable and rewarding if there is no vision and guidance.

Look at the automobile, it cannot go anywhere without a driver. It needs that responsible person to plan and see the road ahead. You also need a suitable designated driver to steer and move you from here to there. I assure you that you will experience the best of life when you have a guide to help you with all your actions, to guide you to reach your desired destination. Vision is the answer. Where do you want to go? Where do you want to be two years from now? How do you see your life, health, finances, and relationships? Are you be happy with the way you are living your life? What will you do to see that your life fulfills its purpose? These questions are not often entertained; in fact, you might not even want to think about them. These questions will help you a great deal if you do not shy away from them. You will be able to dream and see your future exactly how you want it.

Vision and dreams with the right mental attitude give hope to your future. You will have peace of mind knowing that your future is secured. Secured how you may ask? Look when your life is filled with hope there is no way that you will not work out a perfect plan to get your desired results. You simply cannot fail but before you get to hope you must have a vision. Look at it this way, vision is for you to look at your dream with the eyes of "I CAN and THIS CAN BE DONE, or I AM A WINNER."

Once you grasp that you will be filled with the will to act, hope to get up, and make the impossible possible. You will have the superpowers to see beyond tomorrow.

START WITH VISUALISATION, USE YOUR IMAGINATION

We are all born with the power to imagine and to visualize. Most of us intentionally and consciously know how to use our imagination to produce success. All of us visualize or imagine on a daily basis if not every minute. If you are not aware or you are in doubt that you are using creative visualisation every day of your life to influence conditions around you, follow the example below to see if you can relate. Imagine that you are at work sitting by your desk in front of your computer answering telephone calls and responding to emails. Your boss and co-workers come in your office every five minutes to ask if you have completed reports, asking about memos, submissions and when is the next meeting. Your day started with a lot of work that kept you so busy that you forgot to eat lunch.

During the day whilst you busy with your computer typing and reading emails, drafting submissions, and entertaining your boss's demands, you begin to feel hungry. Your mind starts to create pictures and ideas about what you could possibly eat or about something that you ate some time ago that could satisfy the hunger. Your mind shifts from your work to focus on what you will have to eat. You start entertaining pictures of your perfect meal. You start to imagine a sandwich packed with lettuce, beef, ham, cheese, cucumber slices, and some avocado topped with chilli and tomato sauce. In your mind, you start preparing your perfect sandwich.

You imagine how you are going to prepare the sandwich; you know you have all the ingredients. Right there when you are busy preparing your sandwich, your boss just walks into your office asking where the letter she requested from you 20 minutes ago is. There you have it, gone is the picture of your perfect sandwich. After submitting the requested letter, you take two minutes breather, then you begin to think again about what you will eat. This time it is different, you still desire the sandwich but you think you can do better if you eat meat, you think maybe beef steak, salad, and some baked potatoes.

You imagine a home nice grilled steak this time you replace beef with pork steak spinach and add tomato salsa on the side. You are creating that meal in your head. When you do this, you notice that your mood changes, you heighten your craving for food, you become famished and you cannot wait to meet that desire. You become excited because you know you can get such meals. You feel positive because you know you have all the ingredients and tools to prepare your meal. Looking at the above example you did two things, you were using the power to visualize as you read and you proved that you can really use your imagination and visualize.

Exciting don't you think? Now, you get home and begin to prepare your desired sandwich. You are still holding the picture of your sandwich in your head. You pick your white or brown bread, spread your choice of butter on slices of bread, wash your lettuce and tomatoes, and nicely cut them to place between the bread slices and cut your cheese, put ham, and beef burger. Gently with excitement, you spread your perfect choice of sauce on the sandwich, and there you have it. Your meal is ready for eating. Your imagination works, so no excuses, do not ever doubt your ability to visualize.

I am happy that you now have a clearer understanding of what I mean by the power you have within you. Why then do you not use the very same powerful imagination and vision techniques to excel in your career, health, finances, relationships, and any other area of your life? Begin now to use your imagination to create the life you want. Of course, you'll have to exercise and train yourself every day to perfect these techniques and start using them at will. Neuroscientists have proven that when you think or imagine you are altering your life, creating a new reality as you imagine it

As you think in your heart, so are you, the writer of proverbs could have not captured such beautiful words any better. What this simply means is that when you think of something constantly you are creating energy that brings your thought to reality. Think for a moment, everything that you ever wanted, first started with a thought. Perhaps you thought that 'let me wear a red dress to a party,' or 'let me create a painting;' or you are thinking of building a house. All these are thoughts that create pictures of what you want as you think about them. What you can do is to hold that picture long enough in your head and then you will see it materialize. You completed your painting in your mind before you put it on paper; you wore your red dress in your mind first before you put it on your body.

CONTROL THE PICTURES IN YOUR HEAD

Let us have fun together with this one last exercise. Right now, I want you to think about two oranges, one on your left hand and the other on your right hand. Put away the oranges and open your fridge and now close it. Think about the sky; change the whole sky colour to red. Now take the two oranges back into your hands.

Change back the colour of the sky to blue. You see you were controlling what you want to see with your mind.

If you do not control your thoughts consciously your mind will replay old thoughts and images sometimes it will replay bad thoughts and pictures. For you to move away from that you need to consciously control what you see in your head. Always keep pictures that you want to see in your head. Your life will never be the same when you master this technique.

The law of energy says that energy of certain quality attracts energy of similar quality vibrations. What this means is that you need to fill your thoughts, your imagination with the life you want to see, the life you want to live. This principle is experienced when you buy a car then you start seeing the same cars as yours everywhere. Or when everything in your life seems to fall into place or when you think of someone then you accidentally run into that person. You are attracting the same energy vibes that circles in your head.

The above examples and principles are true whether you know them or not. It will be to your advantage for you to know them and learn how to use them to their maximum potential. Now that you are aware of your superpowers, it is time to put it to work in relationships, finances, communication, career, and business. Your success rises and falls on what you think. I am sure by now you understand that your mind through thinking and imagining has a direct and powerful impact on your life.

Remember that Henry Ford said, "Whether you think you can or you think you cannot. Either way, you are right." This goes deeper than thoughts and imaginations. Your feelings also impact your life in the same way. When you constantly choose to feel happy and excited every day you are busy creating the events in your life which will lead you to experience the same happy, exciting emotions.

That is why I will often remind you to think only happy thoughts and remember only happy memories to create thoughts and feelings of the same nature which will then create events of joy. I will also remind you that you are unique and a very capable individual who is perfectly designed to flourish.

By now you already get a hint that your emotions are also a driving force in your life. Your thoughts, imagination, affirmations, and feelings work together, you cannot separate them if you wish to get what you desire. This means that the emotions that you feel will influence your thinking. That is why most people when one thing goes wrong, think of other things that went wrong; then they would affirm such by saying, "nothing ever goes right for me." I will say, check your emotions and your thoughts to fix that. For now, let us not dwell much on that.

We are still focusing on your imaginations and thoughts to creating the life you desire. Your emotions should always be aligned with your thoughts. It is very important to do that. If you do not get the desired results it is probably a connection link between thoughts, imagination, affirmations, and emotions. Always check the connection to make sure that you are on the right track. Feelings and thoughts should speak the same language.

If you have negative thoughts about money, then how are you going to acquire money? Your emotions of having money in abundance should be aligned with your thoughts of abundance. For your creative imagination to take a physical form a goal in mind is a prerequisite. Support your desired goal with beliefs. Your beliefs simply mean come what may, you will not believe anything other than what you know you deserve and want.

You choose to see what you want despite the current circumstances. Support your beliefs with feelings, affirmations, and accepting that which you desire. This reminds me of the words of Christ when he said "whatsoever you desire believe that you have received it and it will be given to you." For you to believe and receive you must keep seeing what no one else sees. Keep that which you want to receive; do not be discouraged if you do not see results right away, I promise that results will come soon. Above all be thankful, show gratitude. Be grateful that you have got everything you desire. "Thought is the only power which can produce tangible riches from the formless Substance," says Wallace Wattle. Follow the below steps, to begin with your exercise.

EXERCISE
Have a desired goal to achieve
For me, it was making R47 000 within a period of two months. My goal was specific, yours should be as well. I wanted R47 000 to clear my debts nothing more. If this is new to you, it is important, to begin with, small goals that you can achieve within a short period so that you gain the momentum of victory. Master this process.

Imagine your desired results
I created my image starting with an idea of what I wanted to achieve. The image you are creating must be specific and of the present moment. This will require you to relax, let go of all your worries, and focus on the goal. I visualized making an extra income of R 5000 every week.

I did not know at that moment, but my goal was clear that at the end of eight weeks I must have R47000, so I visualized myself working day and night to get clients, develop and design websites for them. I just worked and my goal was to pay off my debts in cash. I visualized myself working and not focusing on my debts. I made it my habit to stay positive.

Affirm and experience the emotion of receiving
You do this by constant visualisation, holding the picture in your head every day and every minute until it becomes real. While holding the picture in your head you do not keep quiet, you must

affirm what you want and you express gratitude. What I did was to continue picturing an abundance of cash in my life.

I kept visualizing building good relationships with clients; they paid me well and appreciated my services. I did not keep quiet, I kept affirming. I used Louise L Hay's prosperity affirmation (Please look up Louise L Hay's book, "I CAN DO IT: HOW TO USE AFFIRMATIONS TO CHANGE YOUR LIFE"). As I affirmed, I also made sure that I felt the experience. I went deeper into visualizing as you would when you are watching a movie in 3D.

The pictures I created were so intense and real. That is why there was no chance for me to not get what I wanted. Remember that complaining blocks your affirmations and prevents them from working because a complaint is an affirmation itself, which is why thanksgiving is important.

Give thanks

I gave thanks continuously. I expressed my sincere appreciation for receiving clients, getting paid, and doing a good job. I expressed my deepest appreciation for living in abundance. The thanksgiving stage is a bit tricky, and here is why. some will think you are absolutely crazy by giving thanks for what you do not have.

My answer to this is simple, "FAITH AND TRUST." I had to believe that I am receiving my breakthrough; I made sure that I believed that I am making an extra income of R5000 and more every week. So, for you I will understand if you feel funny at first, I did but my desperation and knowledge drove me to a point of no return. You might feel skeptical also, but give thanks and praise anyway.

You will see the results I promise you. What you are doing is exercising the laws of the universe, specifically the law of cause and effect, the law of attraction, and faith. When you start with the process of imagining it's best if you keep it to yourself until you become comfortable with it.

Others may ridicule you or think you are crazy because they lack knowledge and understanding. You keep at it until you see the results you want. Did I make R5000 every week? You may ask. No, I did not; I did better and made more than what I initially wanted. As I mentioned in part one of my stories, I got clients for web development; they did not pay per week but paid per finished project. My first two projects yielded R37000 in total. I then took a portion of the money to trade on binary stocks.

If you followed my story in part one, you will remember that I mentioned that I was working four jobs in a day. Three of the jobs paid, not so well but the money made a difference, and yes, I reached my target within a period of eight weeks. The events that had followed after the eight weeks were nothing but unparalleled flourishing.

The next page is your space to write your desired end result(s). Work on it as I did above. Make up your own affirmations. Paint a nice picture in your head with colours and put more feeling to it. You will feel great all the time.

GOAL OR DESIRED END RESULTS

Your desired goal should be clear and answer the question "why" You will initiate motivation when you answer "why" and "what"

____

____

____

Imagine your desired results — create your image
Remember that you must put more colour, pictures, and feelings to it. If you do not get it the first time, do it over and over until you feel good about the pictures you are creating.

____

____

____

Experiencing the feeling, Affirm and Believe that you are living that life

Affirm your desired result. Make up your own affirmations per your goal.

____

____

____

Be grateful and give thanks

Remember this is the most critical and important step. You must receive what you desire by giving thanks all the way through.

____

____

____

Hope you enjoyed your exercise

Chapter 19 Seeds Of Life, Goals

Your ability to create is bigger than your current challenges; do not allow hardships to destroy your passion for creating a wonderful life.

This is one of my favourite chapters in the book because it is so practical and simple to understand the effective steps illustrated here. You will get a chance to learn whilst working out your goals, plans, and dreams. At this stage, you acknowledge challenges, change, and crisis but you choose to create a life you deserve because you know you already have all the tools to succeed. The habit to always play defence when you encounter challenging times is gone now; make room to create a living that you will be proud of at the end of your life. Small steps that you take day by day should not be overlooked. If you have a tendency to sometimes get your eyes fixed on problems, it is time to shake that off, remember that it is the everyday small actions that turn into bigger achievements.

The mustard seed, Mark tells us is the smallest seed, but it grows to become the greatest tree that even the birds make their home in it. Everything in the world begins and ends with a seed. Everything in your life begins with; thought, vision, will, goal, and a lot of action until it's done. The laws and principles should be followed; but for you to harvest and enjoy the fruits of your labour, you must begin planting seeds day by day. Plant, take out the weeds and water your seed until it brings forth some real benefits. An example I can make is that of myself, I am a writer; therefore, for you to hold a complete book with good contents I must write and read every day. The knowledge, ideas, and words from my head are seeds to bring forth some written or spoken material.

The words I write do not just come into my head magically; I put them in my head by planting. I read, research, explore, observe, listen, and write over and over again. When I realised that I get joy from writing, I made it a point that a day never passed by without reading and writing. Even if I read and wrote a single, line it was OK, so long as I wrote and read. In the end, that line will add to more writings and eventually become a book, blog post, poem, song or something worth reading.

Some days I did not feel like reading but I read anyway, it is my life's work. That is how you should plant. Of course, your dream or goals are different from mine, learn how I do it, and then apply the principles to your dreams for you to get your desired end results.

BEGIN WITH YOUR GOALS

If I were to ask you right now, what is it that you want, what is your goal? What are you working towards? Would you be able to answer my questions without wavering? If your answer is yes, then you are a step ahead. If your answer is no, then you must really start setting goals now.

Looking from personal experience, I admit that knowing what you want is one long task that is not so "straight forward" to do. You must do it still. It will take time and effort, but be patient and learn about yourself every day as you work your way up. Your life depends on setting goals and knowing what you want. Work on it; do not be discouraged when you do not find it immediately.

It took me five full years for me to truly find that one thing that gives me pleasure and meaning. I jumped from one thing to another until I found out that one thing that matters to me. Am I sure that it is truly what I want? Absolutely not! I am not sure, but I am going to give my best in what I have right now. Dreams and goals are also subject to change. Life changes but that do not mean that you must not set goals or go for what you want. You also do not have to get stuck with those goals. You can change your mind anytime.

Things will become easier with every action you take, look at setting goals as a self-discovery journey that you must enjoy. Through the discoveries, you will get guidance and clarity about your greater purpose. Do not hurry things, with patience everything will work out. If you make setting goals a matter of life and death, pressuring yourself with the process of achieving each and every single detail, you will frustrate yourself, rob yourself of the enjoyment of goal setting and life itself.

Do not be too hard on yourself, and do not take it too seriously. Look at goal setting as an easy guide to putting an order in your life and by prioritizing and getting things done. Most of us go through life blindly without having any specific goal in mind, not knowing what we really want, why we want what we want and how to get what we want.

We charge on towards life without goals and visions. Imagine that you are a hired building constructor, and you do not have any blueprint to guide you specifically on what to build, how, where, with what and how long will it take to complete the building. Do you think you will ever get your job done? I do not think so. Even if you begin, how will you know that you finished your building? Today we will resolve that.

Goals are important in your life, if they do not give you a sense of direction at least they keep you alive. The key is to have goals written down. I will guide you to set up your goals using the well-known "SMART" method that is used in business, I find this method very helpful in personal goals as well. I learned about SMART while studying business administration during varsity days. I know what I am talking about; trust me it works like magic. Once you master the SMART approach, then you can start adjusting the method as you see fit. That is what I did for myself. I learned the principles and then worked my own way of goal setting.

What is this SMART?
SMART
S = Specific
M = Measurable
A = Actionable, attainable, arousing and agreeable
R = Resources, relevant
T= Time
SPECIFIC

Specific, keep it short and simple. It is not a matter of life and death if it does not, but for your sake try to work within the guidelines of the SMART method. The most important thing to start with is that your goal must be specific. For example, if you are going to write a book it is important for you to be specific about the type of book you want to write. Is it going to be fiction, non-fiction, a novel or self-help book?

If you are going to start a shoe business be specific, is it shoes for men, women, or children? If you are opening a bakery you need to be specific about what you are going to bake, is it going to be cheesecake or banana bread? Be specific about your goal. Make your goal statement as short as possible that the next person must understand it as much as you understand it.

MEASURABLE

A Measurable goal allows you to know how far you are in attaining your goal and lets you know when you have achieved your goal. If your goal is to lose weight (30 kg) you must be able to measure how far you are. For example, you might have lost 9kg within two weeks of going to the gym and because your goal is measurable (30kg), you know exactly how far you are from your goal. How many hours per day, per week and per month do you need to work out to achieve the 30kg loss? Measure your intake of carbs and protein intake, calories you want to lose per day.

ACTIONABLE, ATTAINABLE, AROUSING AND AGREEABLE

Action is one ingredient in this approach that you cannot avoid. Not that the others can be avoided but the action is the sweet part. You must take action to see your goals achieved, it is that simple. To gather resources, you need to act; to keep your goals alive, the act of writing them down is important. That goal must be attainable talks to possibility; it means it must be within the measure of reach. Arousing (exciting) simply means your goals should keep you up at night, keep you awake as you cannot stop working on them; be exciting enough that you cannot wait for the morning to come for you to work. The goal must agree with your purpose, development, and skills as a person. If your goal does not agree with righteousness and good it is likely that you will struggle to work on it.

RESOURCE, RELEVANT TO YOUR GOAL

What resources will you need? What do you have so far? When you are constructing a building, you know that you must get bricks, cement, sand, water, windows, doors, tiles, human resources (manpower), and other resources that will complete your house. In my case when I write, I need to read books, do research, use my brain, listen to podcasts, interview people, observe, experiment, and write every day.

Relevancy of resources is important, This also directs you to choose meetings and read books that are relevant to your goals, It helps you to meet, people who will be helping you to get closer to achieving your goals.

TIME

You must be specific about the time frame. Is it going to take you 6 months or 12 months? A goal of over a year or more will affect your performance along the way. That is why in your 4-year course degree there is a breakdown of modules per year or six months so that you know when you make progress. Goals that take more than a year need a different strategy than short-term goals. Therefore, stick to shorter times so that you enjoy the fruits of your labour, build momentum as you get used to the approach. The time setting of your goal will allow you to know how far you are.

NEW YEAR RESOLUTIONS AND BUCKET LISTS DO NOT COUNT

Not everyone takes time to set goals and write them down and also not many people have a clear understanding of how to set goals. I also did not have a clear understanding of setting goals until I did good research on it. New Year resolutions and bucket lists are not goals. How often do you slip off from your New Year resolutions? Do you commit to your bucket list? Most often you do not, therefore stop fooling yourself.

New Year resolutions and bucket lists do not put pressure on you to achieve them. They provide you with no sense of urgency to keep you focused. Forget your New Year resolutions and bucket list and begin working on your goals. Failing to write your goals down may hinder your success in achieving those goals. If you do not write your goals down, you will be just another person doing wishful thinking. It is better to write than to depend on your memory. You simply cannot work out details of each and every goal in your head. You will be forced to write at some point, better do it now.

Bruce Elkin, author, and life coach educates us about goal setting practices. He warns us to not set process goals but results goals. Process goals describe actions, not results and goal results do not only describe the end results but motivates you to begin the work.

HAVE A LOOK AT THESE EXAMPLES:
Process goal: Exercise an hour and 20 minutes each morning, is a process, not a goal, not a result."

Results goal: Become a fit healthier person weighing 50 kg by the end of June 2016.

Process goal: 'Write a book' is a process goal, not a result goal.

Result goal: Publish a 250-word paperback book about gardening

The work involved to achieve the goals is destroying the motivation to start the goal. So, don't put the work (process) first. Put the end result upfront, visualizing fully-completed results that energize you. Below is your chance to put your goals on paper. Use the SMART method and make it relevant to your goals. You must see to it that you follow through with your goal for you to achieve the desired results. If you do not follow through, you will not reap any rewards in the time of harvest.

Allow me to give you another example for you to follow.

Goal
Specific goal: A book of 200 pages about the Nature of birds must be finished by June 2019.

Plan and resources

Your plan could be: Read and research for three hours every day. Your research is to visit zoos, bird museums, bird stores, go to the wild to observe birds, interview experts on the subject of birds, watch TV programs, and read at least 50 books about birds. Write three pages every day and before bedtime, review, and put everything you wrote together into a chapter. Do it one chapter at a time. Although this might be difficult to follow as information about chapters sometimes come spontaneously, in this case, you will need to keep notes for other chapters.

Once you decide about the content you may plan how you are going to publish. Is it going to be with an agency or is it going to be self-publishing? Your marketing plan must be structured. Set out your budget for printing, (perhaps you will start printing 100 books if it is self-published; if it is through publishing companies, they will handle most of the work). With self-publishing, you may also look into your design (book cover and layout) and set the price for your book.

Start planting — Day to day activities
This is the process of your goal. Take the resources listed in the above plan. Read books, do your research to follow, and simply follow through with your entire plan as per time allocated. You would start with the content obviously by writing, and making notes as you read and research.

Watering your seeds
At this stage, you are still writing your three pages a day, reading your books, and researching. With writing, it is simple, because your work to be completed is based on two major things, content and put it on paper. In this process, you will also need proofreading, spell checking, editing, and so on. That's if you are self-publishing. If you have a publisher, you just give your best-written content and the rest will follow.

Reaping the rewards
You have finished the book, now it is selling. As you work on these strategies you learn where to improve, simplify, and embrace the complexity that comes with the reality of hard work.

Your turn...
Goals must be specific
(A fit, healthy weight of XX kg, R10 000 profits every month, a 200-page book on birds, selling shoes for children age 2 – 7, it could be anything you like)

____

____

Plan and Resources

____

____

Planting Stage: Day to day action, putting resources to work

____

____

Watering your seed

____

____

Reaping the rewards

____

____

I imagine that you followed the above example. Right now, I can assure you that you know what to do with your dreams and goals, how to start, who to talk to, and where to begin. What follows is for you to commit and dedicate your life efforts to your goals and dreams.

That challenge that was keeping you awake at night is now gone because you know how to create the life you want through goal setting. That weight that made you frown in the mirror is gone because you know how to get in shape. Your frustrations of not knowing how to become an entrepreneur are gone because you are able to identify resources, tools, contacts that will put you one step closer to owning that restaurant, gym, or book club.

Chapter 20 Keys To Flourish In Times Of Change

"I have known one key to making everything possible and beautiful in life, and that is you."—Rorisang Maimane

Life can be simplified upon your choosing. It is possible to live a life where everything you touch just turns into everything you want. Do you still remember what I did to supplement my income to pay off my debt and start my thriving trade? I made a list of things I know I can do best - skills, talents, and tools I already have. That required a lot of self-analysis and self-examination without judgment. This will be the same for you; you have to know yourself. You have to know what you want.

What is it that you want to do, what is it that you do not want to do. What is it that you want to become, achieve and what results do you expect to produce. Knowing all this will then make it easy for you to reach your goals.

If you do not know what you want to do, do not despair, you will receive all the help you need. Get in touch with me on my email address and I will help you with that. A purpose-driven life is the highest achievement a man can ever accomplish in life. Leading a purpose-driven life makes things easier for you. You know what to do when you wake up, where to go, who to talk to, what resources to look for, which books to read and which talk shows to watch and listen to. Everything you do will be aligned to your purpose; in fact, purpose will guide all your actions. The ultimate key to flourishing in times of change, challenges, and crisis is for you to find out why you exist. Find out your best abilities and use them fully.

If you haven't at least work towards that. You will not master this key if you do not know yourself and understand your best potentials. Knowing yourself will make you fully understand that you are more than just a simple person but a greater being purposely created to make everything you come across shine and grow. Our maker created all beautiful things under the heavens and put you on earth to manage and care for them. When you were created you automatically received all the skills, gifts, powers, resources, and strengths to use so that you can get all the work done. When you know that deep inside you lies the power to do anything, you begin to act with authority over any circumstances. I had this yearning to know why I live; I am sure that you have a yearning to need to know why you exist as well.

This question will be answered by you when you begin to look deep within yourself. I can only guide you through working it out, but most of the work will be from you. James Allen said when a man begins to know, man finds all wisdom, power, and knowledge from within.

Remember that the power of knowledge is one of the tools that will see you through, set you on a beginning pace so that you rise above challenging times. When you are in a constant struggle you suffer. To avoid suffering, you must look for possible elements of ignorance or disobedience to the laws of life. If in some way you do not act right, quickly change that. Your own thoughts, desires, and aspirations form your world. Your suffering is in a way rooted in you, whether in thoughts, deeds, or desires. Beauty, joy, and bliss, or ugliness, sorrow, and pain, all these are contained within yourself. Flourishing life is also rooted in you.

Everything that a man desires is already in him, freedom, love, joy, satisfaction, riches, and power. The same goes for unpleasant desires. They also produce unpleasant circumstances which in some way hurt you. Nothing can just spring out of thin air and be given to you unless there is a seed to produce such fruits. Remember that according to the laws of nature, the process of everything begins with a seed.

Therefore, in you, there are seeds of freedom, love, joy, satisfaction, riches, power and the very strength and knowledge to overcome all challenges in your life. You cannot know this until you fully work on yourself to discover your purpose; your purpose will fill you with powers that are beyond understanding. What will you then do with such powers?

You know that you are a complete person equipped to withstand any form of challenge. That is why when a man discovers his reason for existing, he no longer engages in meaningless activities that will bring him nothing but distress. He focuses on the mission.

When you do what you must do with your life, the universe and the creator somehow find a way to help you. You will never be deprived in any way when you are living out the purpose for which you were created. The author of "In pursuit of purpose", Dr Myles Munroe says "death never scares a person who has discovered his purpose; in fact, when you discover your purpose and fulfill your mission, you welcome death with open arms". Today the reason you are so afraid of small changes and challenges is that you know you have not entered into the course to fulfill the purpose for which you were born.

I strongly believe that each and every single human being in the world has something to add to this world before they depart. What is that gift that you have to present to the world? Yes, we all have gifts and talents. What are yours? It is your job to find out that one gift that you can give to the world before you depart.

Once you find your special qualities, give them to the world by using them to their full potential. Purpose will solve all problems man has. Anything that is outside your purpose will not bother you in any way.

ADDICTED TO FLOURISHING

I want you to be addicted to flourishing like never before, I want you to be a winner wherever you go. Have no room to think negative thoughts, give no room for failure, defeat, and fear. Let flourishing be your walk in your daily life. When you are done with this section it will be impossible for you to talk anything but a victory; it will be a lifestyle for you, you will not think any other way. There is a certain lifestyle that you train yourself to live which will make every situation you face very easy to work on whilst getting the desired end results. I understand that this may be a bit difficult and strange for others to grasp because all they ever knew is the constant struggle to get things right.

The constant fight to have that one breakthrough that will cheer them up and to give them a little room to breathe. That breakthrough that will give them peace in their struggling lives. Believe me, it is possible, I have done it, others have done it and some are doing it. Join the ranks of those who are doing it now so that you may also understand and say that, "I did it as well."

What you need to do is simple. All you have to do now is make a decision to live the lifestyle of unparalleled success. Focus on creating the life you want. The more you give your attention to having a better life, the more your chances multiply to attain the lifestyle of a flourishing individual. Sooner or later this lifestyle will consume you and your thinking, habits, actions, and everything you ever knew about yourself. I want you to learn to train yourself in things that bring you joy, the things that guarantee you a life that you deserve. Learn to walk in the paths that make your life worth living. Let go of defeat and start regaining what is rightfully yours, a flourishing lifestyle.

HOW DO I DEVELOP A FLOURISHING LIFESTYLE?

"Rorisang I hear you, but how?" You may ask how do I achieve this flourishing lifestyle? I am tempted to say read chapter so-and-so or read the book again but good for you I can summarize everything for you and on top of that add some very important guides that will help you. Through degradation and hosting a lot of self-pity parties, I learned a great deal that our personalities, characters, and attitudes are very important in life. In fact, they are the keys to successful living. What you do with your life on a daily basis sets a path for you to walk on in the future. The future is now. I am going to say something that some of you might not like but I will say it all the same because it is true.

IT IS EASY TO CREATE THE LIFE THAT YOU

WANT. Yes, it is easy to develop a flourishing lifestyle. I am not saying that it is not going to take some work. Believe me, it is going to take some effort for you to manifest the desired results. Let us look at addicts, for example, say a drug addict. The minute they direct their attention to the feeling or the end results of taking the drug, their emotions, thoughts, physical behaviour, and vision changes. They fully get absorbed in the allure of taking drugs. What happens then? Desire begins to grow more and more. Dopamine is yearning for feel-good satisfaction. They eventually give in to the feeling. They take the drug and then get the satisfaction they longed for.

The problem is that they will keep wanting more. It is dopamine saying more drugs will give them more satisfaction. It is only natural to want more of what you think is good for you. Imagine using the same principles to get addicted to something good. Something valuable that you can become proud of. Take an example of a writer whose goal is to publish four books within twelve months.

The goal is clear, publish four books within twelve months. They then get addicted to writing and reading. It is that easy. The more you write what you like the more you feel like going. If it is a novel you simply get absorbed in creating your own world. The goal is simple, write, write, and. write. There are other processes involved. The point is to just do it until you see it done. You must have the same craving and desire to move forward and satisfy that urge to succeed. Your goals, your dreams are calling out to you. Will you serve them? When the craving is satisfied, go for more, make it your lifestyle; similar to how an addict goes in search of his next fix. Give yourself enough time to focus your attention on something; it will eventually become part of you through acts, thoughts, and emotions.

PANDORA BOX

Through self-examination with the help of the meeting with myself, I learned of my personality, not knowing that it is the key for me to start rising to new levels. You see your personality is what I call the "Pandora Box," but in this case, your box is full of great attributes, not monsters as we are told according to the Pandora box legend. Your Pandora box is the key to leading a flourishing lifestyle; you simply have to pull out any quality of your choosing as you see fit to the circumstance.

Your personality comprises of all our feelings, thoughts, and behaviours that make you who you are. Let us look at the qualities that come out of our Pandora box. I will only mention those that I am living on a daily basis. I know that there is more. Our differences make it more interesting. The key here is for you to pay close attention to yourself. Learn as much as you can about yourself and then identify your strengths and weaknesses. From there on you will be able to improve accordingly.

ATTITUDE

Attitude is the first gift we start with from the Pandora box. Your attitude is your eyes to the world. With attitude, you can fall or rise, feel good or bad. Attitude gives you all the power you need to begin working out every situation. For example, let us look at the old "glass is half empty or half full" lesson. If you are a person who sees the glass as half-empty, it means you are more likely to complain first about all your challenges. You will be cynical before you finally learn that all the power to flourish is within you. By the time you learn, you would have missed out on a lot of opportunities and wasted time through complaining, hosting pity parties, and asking why me? If you are a person who sees a glass half full, it means you are more likely to get excited realizing that you already have something to build on. You will appreciate what you already have. You will start with plans immediately, assess your chances, and learn as much as possible. You will be very optimistic and in no time, you would accomplish your goals. With this type of attitude, no time is wasted. It is plainly simple that you acknowledge reality and make the best out of what you have.

Your attitude will ultimately build your personality because your attitude is a force from within. It consists of your thoughts, feelings, and beliefs. If I were you I would make sure that my eyes see nothing but a half-full glass all the time, even if it is hard, force yourself to see only beautiful things. This is not a trick because in another world at another time circumstances could be much worse. That is the attitude of a flourishing individual.

PERSONALITY OF A FLOURISHING PERSON AND UNDERSTANDING HOW TO MAXIMIZE YOUR POTENTIALS WITH THIS PERSONALITY

Avery good way to start living a flourishing lifestyle is to understand what a flourishing person does. It is important to identify the strengths and best abilities that lie dormant within yourself. Initiating efforts to train and to walk in paths that guarantee success is another key step. A lot of learning and training in mind and thinking are needed. You must understand how you learn best.

Do you learn well by observing (visual pictures), reading, listening, or what? This way you understand your strengths and direct more attention to your strengths. This is very important for developing a flourishing lifestyle; there can never be a lifestyle without the influence of a personality. This means that we work on your personality and character first, and then the lifestyle will follow.

An excellent way to develop the personality of a flourishing person is to get out and try many new things. You will learn that in doing so you will come across a lot of setbacks and lots of victories. Flourishing personalities do not beat themselves up when they come across setbacks, they get up and try again, keeping the goal in mind, and making sure that they learn as much as possible from the experience.

These personalities have a unique way of handling success, when they do achieve something; they very often do not celebrate that achievement for too long. They already working on the next desired success.

This attitude still gives me goosebumps. I love it because in a way you are conscious of the value of time. You have no time to celebrate one victory. Elon Musk is a perfect example of this personality, he tried everything and done great things. According to the interviews and his documentaries that I watched; Elon has no time to celebrate one success for a very long time.

At least this is my observation from what I gathered by listening to him and watching his interviews. For example, he created PayPal, moved to SpaceX, to Tesla to Solar City, and then to Boring Company. Who could tell what he is up to as I am busy typing here? This is the same with Steve Jobs, he created the Apple, moved to an iMac, and then to the iPod. There is simply no time to waste here.

THINKING WILL GET YOU VERY FAR IF YOU CULTIVATE THE SKILL

I have never met a flourishing person who does not think big, nor have I ever read of any flourishing person who does not think big and cherish the act of thinking. This simply suggests that one way to develop this flourishing personality is to think big at all times. Since you will think, you might as well think big. I heard someone say, "think big yes, but back it up with constant action." While thinking is cherished among flourishing personalities, they also keep big thinkers around. They hang out with big thinkers. You simply cannot hang out with small-time thinkers if you want to be a flourishing personality. Flourishing personalities make sure that they train their thinking by reading, doing research, and always trying to be better than the person they were yesterday.

They are their own measure of success, always chasing their future selves. The idea of hanging around people who sharpen your thinking skills is not a cliché. We all know that thinking is not an easy thing to do. It becomes a lot better and fun when you are around people who think big in every possible way and encourage you to think bigger. This will require you to go out and meet new people, get to new places, and try by all means to get out of your own comfort space. As you set out to meet new people and explore, be careful not to be distracted from your main goals.

FOCUS, FOCUS, AND MORE FOCUS — YOU WILL GET FAR WHEN YOU ARE FOCUSED

This brings us to another quality of flourishing individuals, that is, they are focused and do not let their efforts get distracted. They keep the focus by always writing the main goal down, then revisiting and reshaping it. They are always learning new skills related to the main goal. They dwell in good thoughts, plan, and take strong action. They know that to get ahead they need others who can do things that they cannot do very well, therefore they build successful relationships and partnerships. Flourishing individuals make huge efforts to learn by reading books, listening to tapes, and attending events related to their goals.

They do this for the love of learning, progress, and very often because they value innovation, ideas, and creativity. A flourishing individual knows that learning new things always creates new ideas and possibilities. The attitude of learning is an ongoing process, their love for exploring is astounding. They take time to reflect on their efforts and progress, ask questions, challenge themselves, and they are not afraid of the truth no matter how hard and painful it is to swallow.

Are you a flourishing personality? Do you do any of the above mentioned? It is so true that there are other ways of flourishing. I mentioned strongly at the beginning of the book that there are more ways to prosper in life. You just have to find your best way. I am not concluding that my approach is the only way, but with much boldness and belief, I know for sure that learning what I learned will surely get you somewhere. These are my proposals for you to start with.

As mentioned, because of our differences one may have a very efficient way to get things done without much strain. However, I can boldly argue that the learning attitude is one method that flourishing personalities use. Understanding is the main factor in learning. Without learning and understanding, one cannot accomplish much. If by any chance one accomplishes something without learning and understanding, chances are such accomplishments do not last very long. In such cases, we would say they are lucky. We cannot put our life's work in the basket based on luck. Like any other miraculous thing luck runs out, and then you will end where you began. You might as well start doing things right with understanding because you will need it anyway.

BE AVAILABLE FOR YOUR DREAMS
Author of Internal breakthrough Erick Mokgotho said that he is available to work on his dreams now. He went on to say "what is stopping me to do that? Nothing." Simple words but yet profound, powerful! I am available now. Remember that for as long as you live. Flourishing individuals are available now, they put the effort and let the results do the talking. How committed are you to your dreams? What promise do you make to yourself to keep going no matter what comes?

That diet, new exercise plan, that goal you have been delaying, taking up business classes, working on your communication skills. It can be anything. So long as you show up for it, and honour your soul's need to be free and your heart's desire to be satisfied. Say to yourself that "I will honour my promise to see this dream come true", end of the story. This is key to flourishing. Remember chapter 5, tools in your hands? This has a time element to it. Prioritize your dreams, show up be there. Do the work. Prove yourself worthy of your dreams. I love this one best. Your dreams have to find you working towards something related to the dream as a sign of deserving.

You simply cannot have a dream and then fold your arms wishing it will somehow come true. Join hands with your dreams, strengths, skills, connections, tools, and do not forget to bring your commitment, fire, will, and pure desire to see it through until it is done. Until you get to that level of showing up, to that level where you are available during storms, snows, rain, heat, day and night then you know in your soul that you are not giving your best. Be that someone who is worthy to get what they deserve. You get what you deserve by being available.

This is you simply saying to yourself that you love yourself and value your life and you matter most. You do things that make you feel great about yourself. Things that guarantee success and truly add value. No amount of monetary and corporate success can amount to the level of a person who knows their true value. This only manifests with people who are available to be the best they can be now.

BE A BLESSING
The last important personality of a flourishing personality is that of a giver. Be a giver! I do not know of anyone who is flourishing that does not love to give back. Everywhere you go; it is your duty to give. Giving is not limited to finances or materials. Giving could be many things that can build someone up. You may give of yourself by making time to teach the knowledge you have, support, love, and so on The important thing is that you give no matter what. Take

an example from John D. Rockefeller, the man was a giver. I do not want to repeat the stories about him, it is better to learn about him to understand why I say he is a giver. I understand that you might not be as rich as he was but surely there are some ways that you can give back as I have mentioned.

Develop a lifestyle of giving; I can assure you that when you give, more will be given to you. Giving is an open door to receiving. The writer of Proverbs says that "There are those who [generously] scatter abroad, and yet increase more; there are those who withhold more than is fitting or what is justly due, but it results only in want."

After Word

Your ability to create is bigger than your current challenges; do not allow hardships to destroy your passion for creating a wonderful life.

After reading everything you might think but Rorisang are you saying you no longer have problems or worries? The answer is yes; and if I did have problems perhaps, I did not notice them because I am above those problems. My concern is that most people never experience the joy and great power of overcoming their circumstances, all they have ever known is submitting to their adversities and letting situations become their driving force. This is something that concerns me, so I will reach out to people and help them. If I can help to change just one person's life in a better way, then that person will do the same.

There is an abundance of rewards when you face your challenges with integrity. The Chinese philosophy, "Yin and Yang" has a great and powerful approach to life that every one of us must learn and then apply to face life's changes. This "Yin and Ying" philosophy simply says that in life there are two sides to every situation. Life throws challenges at you but at the very same time, there are opportunities equal or greater to the challenges. If you begin to use this approach to all your life circumstances, you will flourish in the face of all your challenges. When others are crying about job losses, you start a business for yourself, when others fear, worry, and become restless you become calm, confident, and work your way up to greater things. The economy of the world will not affect you; you will have financial prosperity and an abundance of good rewards will shower your life endlessly. Some challenges are tests when the testing period is done, you will never be the same person again.

Appendix A

Do you want to write and publish your own book?
Publishing a book will help you to:
Market your business
Attract more clients
Earn extra income
Share your stories, ideas, and passion(s) the world
Put you in the position of an expert Attract potential opportunities

Give you a sense of purpose and importance
Get in touch, find out how we can work together to get your books published. Remember "if you can think it and talk about it, you can also write it"

CREATE THE LIFE YOU WANT

Identify your skills and rediscover your gifts and potentials and begin to create what matters to live a fulfilling life you deserve. Do you want to know what you were born to do? Your purpose and why you are here? There is help available for you, begin now to discover your purpose and work on your skills to create a flourishing life! If you already identified your skills but do not know what to do, I can help you capitalize on them and live up to your full potentials. It is important for you to discover your purpose and skills early. Doing so will benefit you tremendously. Your skills can pay you.

You will have peace and a sense of meaning.

You will live life on your own terms.

Get in touch with, find out how we can work together.

Email: rorisang@helpmyworld.co.za
www.rorisangmaimane.co.za
www.helpmyworldpublishing.co.za
www.helpmyworld.co.za

Bibliography

Anette Prehn, 2012. Play Your Brain: Adopt a Musical Mindset and Change your Life and Career. Edition. Marshall Cavendish Corp/Ccb.

Brainey Quote. Albert Einstein Quotes. [ONLINE] Availablesat:https://www.brainyquote.com/quotes/quotes/a/albertei ns131187. html. [Accessed 5 December 2016].

Bruce Elkin, 2012. THE ABCs of emotional mastery.

Caroline Leaf, 2013. Switch on Your Brain: The Key to Peak Happiness, Thinking, and Health. 8.2.2013 Edition. Baker Books.

Dan James. 2015. A Big Creative Yes to the creativity within. [ONLINE] Available at: http://coachcreative.com/abigcreativeyes/.[Accessed 1 January 2017].

Debt Rescue. 2016. Shaming of poor South Africans does all citizens a disservice. [ONLINE] Available at:http://debtrescue.co.za/apress/shaming-of-poor-south-africans-does-all-citizens-a-disservice/.[Accessed 29 February 2016].

George S. Clason, 1989. The Richest Man in Babylon. Reprint Edition. Penguin Books USA, Inc.

Gerry Robert, 2007. The Millionaire Mindset: How Ordinary People Can Create Extraordinary Income. Edition. Life success Publishing.

Graeber, D, 2011. Debt: the first 5000 years. New York: Melville House Publishing.

James Allen, 2007. All These Things Added. Edition. Cosimo Classics. James Allen, 2007. Light on Life's Difficulties. Edition. Cosimo Classics.

Kenneth Copeland and Gloria Copeland, 2011. From Faith to Faith. Edition. Harrison House Publishers.

Kenneth Copeland, 2012. The Laws of Prosperity. Edition. Harrison House Publishers.

Lord of War, 2005. [DVD] Andrew Niccol, United States: Lionsgate. Marianne Williamson, 2009. A Return to Love: Reflections on the Principles of a Course in Miracles. Abridged Edition. HarperOne.

Meyer, J, 2013. Financial Management God's Way. 1st ed. United States of America.: Joyce Meyer Ministries.

Munroe, M, 2011. Understanding Your Place in God's Kingdom: Your Original Purpose for Existence. U.S.A: Destiny Image®Publishers, Inc.

Rocky Balboa. (2006). Rocky Balboa's inspirational speech to his son. [Online Video]. 6 February 2008. Available from: https://www.youtube.com/watch?v=_Z5OookwOoY. [Accessed: 1 April 2016].

Schwartz, D J, 2012. The magic of thinking big. 1st ed. United Kingdom: Ebury Publishing.

Succeedfeed Quote. Simon Sinek Quotes. [ONLINE] Available at: http://succeedfeed.com/100-amazing-simon-sinek-quotes/ [Accessed 19 August 2017].

Sutton, G, 2004. The ABCs of Getting Out of Debt: Turn Bad Debt into Good Debt and Bad. 1st ed. United State: RDA Press.

The Board of Wisdom Board of Wisdom. A Favorite of 1 user.[ONLINE]Availableat:http://boardofwisdom.com/togo/Quotes /ShowQuote/?msgid=426610 [Accessed 14 January 2017].

Torabi, F, 2010. Psych Yourself Rich: Get the Mindset and Discipline You Need to Build Your Financial Life. United State: Pearson Education.

USAID from the American people. 2013. Education: The Most Powerful Weapon for Changing the World. [ONLINE] Available at: https://blog.usaid.gov/2013/04/education-the-most-powerful-weapon/. [Accessed 9 August 2016].

Wallace D Wattles, 2015. The Science of Getting Rich: How to make money and get the life you want. 1 Edition. CreateSpace Independent Publishing Platform.

9 780620 745444